r '01-97   DD.14.95

THE HUNT *and* THE FEAST

A Life of Ernest Hemingway

THE HUNT

and

THE FEAST

A Life of Ernest Hemingway

• • • • • • • •

By John Tessitore

An Impact Biography

FRANKLIN WATTS   *A Division of Grolier Publishing*
New York · London · Hong Kong · Sydney · Danbury, Connecticut

For my friend Gabriel Piedrahita,
a true aficionado

•   •   •   •   •   •

Thanks to my parents, my sisters, and Kelly
for their patience, encouragement and love.

Photographs ©: A. E. Hotchner: 169; Archive Photos: 30, 64, 76, 82, 86, 88, 143, 177, 190, 192; Bettmann Archive: 66; Brown Brothers: 45, 56, 115; Culver Pictures: 165; The Ernest Hemingway Foundation of Oak Park: 8, 13, 22, 50; The Historical Society of Oak Park & River Forest: 28; Jay Mallin: 173; John Fitzgerald Kennedy Library: 17, 24, 26, 32, 33, 38, 41, 53, 59, 60, 63, 74, 80, 81, 101, 103, 110, 140, 181, 195, 205,; Library of Congress/Amercian Red Cross: 43; Life Magazine © Time Inc.: 154 (David Scherman); Magnum Photos:, 2, 57, 132 (all photos Robert Capa), 188 (Andrew St. George); Princeton University Libraries, Department of Rare Books and Special Collections: 70, 91; UPI/Bettmann: 122, 148, 160, 161, 163, 182, 199.

Library of Congress Cataloging-in-Publication Data
Tessitore, John.
    The hunt and the feast : a life of Ernest Hemingway / by John Tessitore.
        p.   cm. — (An Impact biography)
    Includes bibliographical references and index.
    Summary: A biography of the acclaimed American writer whose childhood and adult experiences became common themes in his stories and novels.
    ISBN 0-531-11289-6
    I. Hemingway, Ernest, 1899–1961—Juvenile literature. 2. Authors, American— 20th century—Biography—Juvenile literature.
    [1. Hemingway, Ernest, 1899–1961. 2. Authors, American.]
    I. Title.
    PS3515.E37Z8918   1996
    813'.52—dc20
    [B]   96-24325
                                                                        CIP
                                                                        AC

TABLE OF CONTENTS

THE SPOILS OF WAR

CHAPTER I

Coming along the road on a bicycle, getting off to push the machine when the surface of the road became too broken, Nicholas Adams saw what had happened by the position of the dead.

— A Way You'll Never Be

A PERSON CAN rarely point to a moment in his life and say for sure that it, more than any other moment, shaped his entire future. But for Ernest Hemingway, the night of June 7, 1918 provided one of those moments. Lying in an exploded foxhole at a point on the Italian front nearest to enemy lines, with the sounds of battle erupting all around him, the nineteen-year-old Hemingway found the action for which he had been searching. Weeks earlier, in his haste to join the war effort, he may not have considered all that war entailed. But now, in the trenches, he knew what war was. He had learned the hard way. And he almost learned too late. He was wounded, his legs were bleeding badly, and a dead man lay not three feet away. Another man, also wounded, was moaning somewhere close by. Heavy-artillery shells and machine-gun fire lit up the night sky. Slipping in and out of consciousness, Hemingway had to wait for a friendly soldier to pull him out of no-man's-land.

7

Hemingway in 1918. That year, while serving in an Italian volunteer ambulance unit, Hemingway was severely wounded near the Austrian front.

Few men of any age have the opportunity to prove themselves on such an epic stage. But the Italian countryside during World War I was, in fact, Hemingway's proving ground. Hemingway had entered the global conflict on his own terms in 1918. After decades of neutrality, America joined the Allied powers in April of the previous year. As a young, Kansas City newspaper reporter fresh out of high school, Hemingway could not keep his mind off of the action. He volunteered for the army in 1917 but failed his physical and was rejected because of an eye defect. Kept from the real action of the European battleground, Hemingway pursued his reporting job with great intensity. Sometimes it seemed as if he approached his job as a substitute battlefield. He insisted on having the tough assignments and the big stories, preferring to cover incidents of violence to everything else. His fearlessness, and recklessness, instantly drew the attention of his peers. "He wanted to ride ambulances," a fellow reporter at the *Kansas City Star* once remarked.[1] But since ambulances and violence were what the young adventurer wanted, he soon grew impatient as a reporter in the relatively peaceful Midwest. The battle spreading across Europe was calling him with a much louder voice. He was ashamed of his peaceful life in the States while his peers and countrymen were across the Atlantic Ocean risking their lives. So in 1918, he found a way to enter the heroic universe of world war.

Hemingway was always an avid reader, almost as bookish as he was adventuresome, and his reading influenced the way he saw himself in relation to the rest of the world. In 1917, just as his impatience to enter the war was reaching a climax, he came upon Hugh Walpole's novel *The Dark Forest*, an account of an ambulance driver's life during war. The excitement and romance that Walpole vividly described in his book immediately appealed to the young reporter's sense of duty and his thirst for action. He wasted no time in following his fancies. In January, he volunteered to join the Red Cross relief efforts in Italy. The Red Cross ignored his defective eyesight, and he was soon accepted as an ambulance driver, of all things.

After a long journey across the ocean, Hemingway arrived in France in June and immediately had his first war adventure. On his way to Paris during that first night, Hemingway and another Red Cross recruit were delayed somewhere in Bordeaux. Paris was under attack; the Germans were shelling the city heavily using an enormous siege canon known as "Big Bertha."[2] French authorities tried to prevent anyone from entering or leaving the city limits. But Hemingway, in his haste to join the action, ignored the good sense of his companion and hired a taxi to take him to the place of heaviest bombardment. He must have paid the driver quite a sum for such a dangerous joyride. That night, he watched excitedly as bombs dropped all around him.

Hemingway's Red Cross unit, Section IV, was to be stationed in Schio in the northeast of Italy, not far from Venice. Its main task was to service the Italian army, whose duty to defend the countryside grew more difficult by the day. Eight months earlier in October, the Germans and Austrians threatened the Italian war effort with an assault on the lines at Caporetto, pushing the Italians back seventy miles to the towns of Tagliamento and Schio and the shores of the Piave River. This offensive jeopardized most of the Italian manufacturing industries centered on Venice. The stakes were high for both sides, as Italian involvement in the war hung in the balance. In this strategically critical part of the world, Hemingway learned about warfare and gathered the stories he would later use in his greatest works of fiction.

Stopping in Milan before reaching their base of operations in Schio, Hemingway and Section IV received their first orders for a relief mission. A munitions factory in the city had exploded, leaving a great number of dead bodies lying in the rubble of the disintegrated building. The recruits were directed to collect the dead as they searched for survivors. The charred bodies and separated limbs that Hemingway found among the fragments of the blast affected him so deeply that he came back to them later, in one of the most moving scenes of his story "A Natural History of the Dead":

> *The picking up of the fragments [was] an extraordinary business; it being amazing that the human body should be blown into pieces which exploded along no anatomical lines. . .*[3]

Once in Schio, the recruits were paired with veteran drivers so that they could learn both the routine for removing the wounded (and dead) from the battlefields and the windings of poor country roads, which demanded that they be alert and skillful drivers. Hemingway enjoyed the first few weeks of his war experience immensely. On his days off he would borrow a Ford ambulance and drive through the countryside with fellow recruit Bill Horne, who remained a close friend of the writer after the war. Together, they explored the countryside, learned the customs of its people, and found the best places to fish. But his fondness for action, the very thing that brought him to Italy in the first place, mostly proved to be an obstacle to making friends. The veteran drivers were particularly distrustful of him, believing that his youthful recklessness put Section IV in danger. As veteran driver Emmett Shaw later said:

> *And Hemingway, we didn't like him and he didn't like us...We liked to swim. We liked to bathe. But not him. He wanted action. He wanted to "participate in the struggle." He thought we were a bunch of do-nothings. On our part, we thought he was an impulsively presumptuous child come to endanger our nice life at Schio.*[4]

As a result of such hostility, there were probably few tears shed among the veterans when the loose-cannon Hemingway volunteered for a new and more dangerous duty at the end of his first month in action. In late June, Red Cross Captain James Gamble selected Hemingway, Bill Horne, and six other young drivers for the "rolling canteens" detail. Their job was to boost the morale of the Italian troops by delivering cigarettes, chocolates, writing paper, clean water, and magazines directly to the trenches.

With a helmet, a gas mask, and a sack filled with things for the troops, Hemingway would bicycle across the bombarded Italian lines to make his deliveries. Finally he found himself in the thick of the action. He enjoyed the danger of this work and succeeded in making a name for himself as a courageous man. During this period, he came to be known among the Italians as *"giovanni Americano,"* the "cheerful American."[5] And the Italians needed all the cheer they could get. The Austrians had begun a new, bloody offensive on June 15. While the lines were holding, there was intense fighting throughout the Piave river region. For Hemingway, if not for the Italians, the worst was still to come. But the worst in this case proved to be a kind of mixed blessing, an event that combined intense physical pain with the possibility for great honor.

July 7, 1918 was a hot, sticky day. The Italian troops crouched in their dugouts, alert and watchful after hearing reports of an imminent Austrian offensive against the Piave region closer to Schio. Hemingway fulfilled his duties that day just as he had on every other day. But he sensed the tension building among the men in the trenches. He knew that a battle was coming, and he wanted to be involved.

He returned to the lines that night, still waiting for the action to start. He even received permission to visit with the two men squatting in the advanced listening post, a hole in the ground 150 yards closer to the Austrian lines. The night was so dark that he only found these men by following the glow of their radium watches across the empty field.[6] He was as close to the Austrians as he could possibly be when they attacked. At half past midnight, the bombardment began. Rifle and machine-gun fire and exploding shells filled the air with a deafening noise. And then came the noise that Hemingway described in *A Farewell to Arms*, the "chuh-chuh-chuh-chuh" of an approaching shell, "then there was a flash, as when a blast furnace door is swung open."[7]

Hemingway was hit. A trench mortar had fallen directly into the hole where he sat with the two soldiers. One of the men was dead, his legs blown off. The other was severely wounded by pieces of shrapnel in his chest. Hemingway could not move, either. Later, he would learn about the 227 pieces of shrapnel that were lodged in his legs. But for now, all he knew was that he was bleeding badly and that his body was feeling increasingly heavy. Soon, he was barely conscious from the loss of blood.

At some point during the constant shelling that night, Italian soldiers reached the advanced listening station and pulled Hemingway and the two other men from the rubble. Placed on a stretcher, he was carried across the battlefield and was dropped to the ground a few times by his carriers as the shells fell close to their path. Once behind the Italian lines, he was put on an ambulance. Now on the other side of the driver's seat, hurting badly, he cursed the familiar roads to the dressing station at Fornaci. Every bump was jarring and caused him excruciating pain. At Fornaci, medical workers separated the wounded from the dead and accomplished only the quickest, most rudimentary medical procedures. For Hemingway, they could only extract the largest pieces of

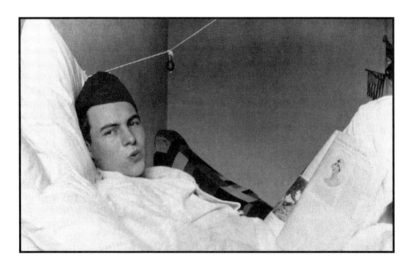

Hemingway recuperates in a hospital near Milan, Italy, in 1918. For his bravery on the battlefield, Hemingway was decorated by the Italian government.

shrapnel from his legs. Then he was put back on an ambulance and driven to the field hospital at Treviso. He stayed in Treviso for a few days, while doctors removed more of the shrapnel and kept his legs in bandages, watching for the onset of infection. There was no need to worry, however, because the metal shrapnel was so hot upon entering his legs that the wound was effectively sterilized.[8] Finally, a little over a month after arriving in Italy, Hemingway's combat experiences were over, and he was taken to a new American hospital in Milan to recuperate from his wounds.

But, however brief his war experience had been, it had a profound effect on the young man and future writer. The Hemingway mystique was beginning to take shape. The Great War demanded self-sufficiency and courage from its participants, reinforcing qualities that young Hemingway was already seeking on his own when he arrived at Schio. These qualities formed a code of behavior that would direct the events of his life, pervade his works, and serve as a philosophical guide for an entire generation of his American readers and the multitude of writers who copied his style. He survived where many other men had failed to survive. He now thought of himself as a man of action, and a superior one because he had lived to tell about his experiences. And when the real-life circumstances of his war involvement failed to represent that superiority in any way, he would make up events and present himself more favorably in the public eye. If his scarred legs failed to bring him the respect of his peers, then he would tell them that he was a war hero, that he had saved lives, that he had been an active soldier, that he had been shot. He was not afraid to lie for recognition. Thus, following the war, Ernest Hemingway embarked on a career of self-glorification that would almost be as important as his writing career for bringing him unprecedented international celebrity.

But even if he lied about himself as a public figure, his art remained almost brutally pure. Ironically, if the truth about

Hemingway's life can be found anywhere, it is found only by piecing together the autobiographical elements of his fiction. His World War I experiences appear in many of his novels and a good number of his short stories. Indeed, the war and the fateful night of July 7, 1918 marked the beginning of his life as an adult and provided material for his most mature work. From that night on, his childish enthusiasm for action and first-hand experience would be channeled, at least partially, into his efforts as a fiction writer. If he spent his life as a public figure promoting his own bravery and skill, his writing about the war was free from his myth-making impulses. In fact, his fictional accounts of the war are always disillusioning about concepts like heroism and honor. Hemingway seems never to have found the glory he sought in combat as a daring nineteen-year-old ambulance driver. But he always went back to the battlefield, always searching for that elusive glory. As the poet Archibald MacLeish wrote on his friend Hemingway's death in 1961:

> *What he took part in was a public—even a universal—history of wars and animals and gigantic fish. And he did take part. He could never go to war—and he went to every war available to him—without engaging in it.*[9]

AN AMERICAN STORY

CHAPTER II

He would be standing with his father on one shore of the lake, his own eyes were very good then, and his father would say, "They've run up the flag."
—*Fathers and Sons*

RNEST HEMINGWAY WAS in some way connected to most of the important events of the early twentieth century. Sometimes he would seek out the action, and sometimes the action would doggedly seek him out. But he was there in the thick of things for nearly five decades, through war, peace, wealth, poverty, happiness, and despair until his death in 1961. His constant presence in twentieth-century history is somewhat less surprising, however, when one considers that he is only the most famous member of a family that participated in all of the important events in American history.

His paternal grandfather, Anson Tyler Hemingway, was born in 1844 in East Plymouth, Connecticut, a descendant of Jacob Hemingway, a patriot soldier in the American Revolution. Anson could even trace his lineage in America back to Ralph Hemingway, who settled in Duxbury, Massachusetts, in 1633, thirteen years after the Pilgrims landed at Plymouth Rock. The son of a clock salesman,

The son of Clarence Edmonds Hemingway (known as Ed) and Grace Hall Hemingway, Ernest Hemingway was born on July 21, 1899 in Oak Park, Illinois.

Anson had a relatively comfortable and peaceful childhood—peaceful at least until 1861. In that year, with the nation divided between the North and the South over the question of slavery, the first shots were fired on Fort Sumter in South Carolina and the American Civil War began. Young Anson enlisted in the Union army, in the Seventy-Second Illinois Infantry, and by 1863, he had fought in a number of important battles, including the battle of Vicksburg under General Ulysses S. Grant, the future eighteenth president of the United States.

After the war, Anson attended Wheaton College in

Illinois where he met Adelaide Edmonds, a botanist and amateur astronomer who was also attending Wheaton. They were married after graduation. Both were firm believers in the value of education and would later send all six of their children to Oberlin College. Anson was a deeply religious man and a friend and supporter of the Protestant evangelist Dwight Moody. Moody was president of the Chicago chapter of the Young Men's Christian Association (YMCA), and Anson served as his secretary until he found that he could not support his family on the YMCA's meager salary. He therefore shifted occupations and found success in the real estate business. Indeed, Anson became so successful that he could soon afford a house in Oak Park, one of the most exclusive suburbs of Chicago. Anson Hemingway's house, at 444 North Oak Park Avenue, was a dark, clapboard structure that looked as plain and as serious as its religious owner.

Across the street, at 439 North Oak Park Avenue, lived the man who would later become Ernest Hemingway's maternal grandfather, Ernest Hall. Hall was born in Sheffield, England, the child of a silversmith. As a young boy, he immigrated with his family to a farm in Dyersville, Iowa. But farm life did not appeal to the spirited young man, and he ran away to Mississippi at the first opportunity. Hall returned to Iowa in April of 1862, not because he disliked the life he had created for himself as a day laborer in the river towns along the Mississippi, but because he too wanted to fight in the Civil War. He enlisted in the First Iowa Volunteer Cavalry and fought for the Union after the war had escalated and the North had experienced numerous early defeats. Like Anson Hemingway, Ernest Hall saw his share of action and was wounded in Warrensburg, Missouri. He carried a bullet in his leg for the rest of his life. The stories his grandfathers would later tell about their Civil War experiences left a deep impression in Ernest Hemingway's mind, a longing for action as well as a profound respect for veterans of combat. As a middle-aged man, he would write:

[War] was one of the major subjects and certainly one of the hardest to write truly of and those writers who had not seen it were always very jealous and tried to make it seem unimportant, or abnormal, or a disease as a subject, while, really, it was just something quite irreplaceable that they had missed. . . Civil war is the best war for a writer, the most complete.[1]

Ernest Hemingway would see more than his share of combat, sometimes as a participant, and would write about it all skillfully. But he would always use his grandfathers' bloody and glorious war experiences as the standard for his own observations.

Ernest Hall married Caroline Hancock soon after the war and moved to Chicago to work in his brother-in-law's cutlery business. Caroline, a painter and an accomplished pianist, was a fine match for her spirited, impressive husband. (Ernest Hall was such a powerful figure in his own home that his grandchildren called him "Abba"—the Hebrew word for "father" and a Biblical term of respect.) Together, Ernest and Caroline moved into a dark, three-floored Victorian home at 439 North Oak Park Avenue that was as illustrative of the Halls' majestic qualities as the clapboard house across the street was appropriate to the Hemingways' religious fervor. The Hall house was grand, stately, and fashionable in the late-nineteenth-century style. It was one of the first houses in the Chicago suburbs to have a telephone.

Caroline's love of music and Ernest Hall's interest in cultured, comfortable living created an atmosphere in which their first child, Grace, could pursue her true passion, the opera. Born in 1872, and trained throughout her childhood as a contralto, the lowest female voice part, Grace Hall was a successful music teacher and a rising performer who debuted in New York in 1895 in an operatic performance at Madison Square Garden. Her future as a singer seemed very promising by the time she reached her twenty-fourth birthday. She had signed on with the world-renowned Metropolitan Opera

Company and might have gone far, to leading roles and perhaps even stardom. But her plans changed when she renewed an old acquaintance with Anson Hemingway's son, Clarence Edmonds Hemingway, the quiet boy across the street.

Clarence, known as Ed, was a young doctor just out of Oberlin College and Rush Medical School in Chicago. When he and Grace met again, Ed was assisting Dr. William Lewis, who was treating Grace's mother Caroline for terminal cancer. Ed was a large-framed, serious young man with deep-set eyes, a lover of the outdoors who periodically searched the surrounding countryside for relics of Native American camps. In later years, he would rise through his profession to become a very influential physician and the head obstetrician at Oak Park Hospital. But in 1894, he was just an intelligent young man with strong religious beliefs and a compassionate heart for the sick. Marcelline Hemingway, Ernest's older sister, would remember her father as a caring healer:

> From the time he was a small boy, my father's emotions were touched by the need of any wounded bird or animal, and he used to put splints on a wounded creature's leg or wing.[2]

Perhaps it was his compassion that attracted Grace at that difficult time in her life. The two certainly made an unlikely pair, like their houses on North Oak Park Avenue. Grace was vivacious and artistic. Ed was sober and rugged. But soon they were very close friends and remained inseparable after Caroline Hall's death. On October 1, 1896, they were married at Oak Park First Congregational Church, and Ed moved into the spacious Hall house to live with his new bride and her family. By that time, Grace had already given up her opera career so that she could live a more conventional life with her husband and the children she expected to have. But she would never be a conventional housewife, and she would continue to give music lessons to neighborhood children even after her own children were born.

Ernest Miller Hemingway was born in his mother's Oak Park bedroom on July 21, 1899, the second of the Hemingway children. As in Grace's five other pregnancies, Ed was the doctor who presided over the delivery. (The other five children were, in order, Marcelline, born in 1898; Ursula in 1902; Madelaine or "Sunny" in 1904; Carol in 1911; and Leicester in 1915.) Baby Ernest was a healthy nine and a half pounds and was named after his grandfather Ernest Hall. Only a year separated Ernest from his older sister Marcelline, allowing Grace to fulfill an odd wish that she had during her first few years of motherhood. Marcelline remembers:

> *Mother often told me she had always wanted twins, and that though I was a little over a year older than Ernest ... she was determined to have us be as much like twins as possible.*[3]

Grace, therefore, dressed Ernest in frilly outfits to match his sister's clothes, a common practice in the Victorian era of the late nineteenth century. But there would be no mistaking Ernest's masculinity in the early years. As a child, he displayed signs of the robust, physical personality for which he would be known later in life. In a keepsake album in which she recorded her memories and kept pictures of Ernest throughout his childhood, Grace recorded that Ernest "comes and slaps you if you don't suit him and kisses you when he is sorry."[4] Grace also recorded Ernest's first spoken word as "Papa,"[5] no doubt referring to Ed Hemingway at the time, but predicting the nickname by which Ernest himself would be known through most of his adult life.

For most of Ernest's childhood, the Hemingways lived in Abba Hall's house at 439 North Oak Park Avenue. It was a household that valued its family history and enjoyed good stories. Abba Hall was a well-traveled veteran of combat with a flare for recounting his experiences. But, as Marcelline remembers, his stories left deep impressions in the minds of his oldest grandchildren even when they didn't involve the war:

The Hemingway home in Oak Park, Illinois

*Abba would tell Ernest and me stories about a pack of little dogs who
had a series of exciting adventures. He would add to this tale endlessly.
Other times he told us about the old days in Chicago, when he rode on
the horsecars, or of his early life on the farm in Iowa, which he hated.
Once he told us about meeting Charles Dickens on one of his walks
about London years before.[6]*

Also living in the Hall house were Grace's younger brother
Leicester and Abba's brother-in-law Benjamin Tyley Hancock.
Uncle Tyley was a door-to-door salesman and, on his
stopovers in Oak Park, he too was full of interesting stories
about his experiences in the American heartland. Ernest
absorbed the stories with great interest and was soon testing
his own abilities as a storyteller. One day, after young Ernest
claimed to have caught a runaway horse all by himself, Abba

Hall turned to Grace and said, "This boy is going to be heard from some day. If he uses his imagination for good purposes, he'll be famous, but if he starts the wrong way, with all his energy, he'll end in jail."[7] What Abba didn't know was that Ernest would use his imagination in both ways. It certainly made him famous, but his talent for storytelling, and even lying, would get him into a little trouble as well.

Later in life, Hemingway would be critical of his Oak Park childhood. As a religious, conservative community that frowned upon ostentation of any kind and would not even tolerate the establishment of a store for the sale of alcohol, Oak Park seemed too restrictive and dull for the adventurous young boy. "I once had a wonderful novel to write about Oak Park and would never do it because I did not want to hurt living people," Hemingway would say later in life.[8] Needless to say, the book would not have been flattering. But Grace and Ed Hemingway did what they could to expand their children's horizons. Grace encouraged Marcelline and Ernest to take dancing classes, even though Ed and most of Oak Park frowned on such frivolous pastimes. And Ed took special pride in the outdoor education that his children received every summer at the family cottage along the northern coast of Lake Michigan in Harbor Springs, Michigan.

The Hemingway summer retreat, called Windemere, was situated a few miles inland from the Great Lake, on the smaller Walloon Lake near Traverse Bay. It would be the future setting of many of Ernest's greatest short stories, especially the early Nick Adams stories. Nearby, was a camp of Native Americans from the Ojibwa tribe, leather tanners who would also appear later in some of Hemingway's best fiction. Windemere was an active boy's dream. Young Ernest could swim in the lake, camp out on the shore at night, hike through the dense forest wilderness, go fishing, and, of course, hunt with his father.

Ed might have been a caring healer by nature and profes-

Ernest (left) and his sisters Ursula and Marcelline look on as their mother displays her catch of the day, a pike, on the shore of Walloon Lake, Michigan, where the Hemingways spent many summers.

sion, but with a rifle in his hand, he was an expert marksman and an avid hunter, even breaking the law at times to hunt out of season. Ed took Ernest fishing for his third birthday and soon had his son loading and firing his own rifle. The outdoor life suited young Ernest. His hero during his early years was Theodore Roosevelt, president of the United States until Ernest was eleven years old.[9] Teddy, as he was known throughout the nation, was renowned for his numerous displays of courage and for his image as an outdoorsman—or for his active involvement with the "Rough Riders" during the Spanish-American War, for the incredible physical strength he displayed when he finished a speech after an assassination attempt left him wounded, and for the numerous safari expeditions he led, hunting big game through Africa and South America as a fifty-two-year-old ex-president. In her keepsake album, Grace noted the Roosevelt-like demeanor of her son, even at a very early age:

> [*Ernest*] *delights in shooting imaginary wolves, bears, lions, buffalo, etc. Also he likes to pretend he is a* "*soldser*"*. . .He is perfectly fearless. When asked what he is afraid of, he shouts out* "*fraid of nothing*" *with great gusto.*[10]

This " 'fraid of nothing" attitude would later become a part of Hemingway's code running through most of his fiction, along with the hunting and war themes in which he delighted as a child.

Back in Oak Park, the Hemingways did not live a lifestyle very common to suburban America at the turn of the century. Grace was not a homemaker as most women were in that era. She hired young girls from Chicago to do the housework and take care of the children. Ed helped out with the cooking and the household chores after he finished his day at the hospital, while Grace organized church choirs, taught her music students, and involved herself in some of the more pressing social issues of the day. She was interested in the work of Jane Addams, who organized Hull House, a settlement house in Chicago helping inner-city immigrants survive in the New World. She helped the suffragettes, women who were fighting for the right to vote. And at Walloon Lake she was more active physically than the average woman and mother was in the early 1900s. She often accompanied her children on their fishing trips and even had a rifle of her own so that she too could enjoy the hunting season.

By 1909, Grace was convinced that her family had outgrown the Hall house in which she had grown up. Abba Hall

Ed and Grace Hemingway with their children, (left to right) Ernest, Ursula, Sunny, and Marcelline, in 1910.

had died in 1905 of nephritis, a painful form of kidney failure, and the family was distraught and sorely missed the grandfather's lively, dignified presence in the old, Victorian rooms. But after a long mourning period, Grace decided that it was time for her family to move on; and in Grace's mind, moving on implied moving into a bigger and more luxurious home. For some time, she labored over her own plans for a dream house. Heavily influenced by the new, purely American, "Prairie" architecture pioneered by another famous Oak Park resident, architect Frank Lloyd Wright, Grace designed an enormous mansion to be built at 600 North Kenilworth Avenue. The house contained a room for each of the six

Hemingway children as well as two rooms for servants, an office for Ed, and a music conservatory for Grace and her music students that was large enough to hold one hundred people for performances.

All of the Hemingway children were now expected to take part in the musical life of Grace's house. Young Ernest, though he displayed little musical ability, played the cello in family performances and later in his high school orchestra. But he was also devoting his energy to activities for which he was better suited. At Oak Park and River Forest Township High School, Ernest tried very hard to be an athlete. He played for the football and water polo teams, swam, and ran track. But he was a large boy and, though growing increasingly handsome, he was awkward and had difficulty keeping up with faster and more agile opponents. Awkwardness would continue to plague Hemingway throughout his life, resulting in a number of accidents, some minor and some major, and a few painful and persistent injuries.

For the most part, he had an easier time using his talents in the classroom than he did on the playing field. He was a well-rounded, solid student, excelling in English and history. And he proved his abilities with a pen at an early age. Even though he lived an active, sportsman's life with his father's encouragement, Ernest was a voracious reader and read everything he could find in his parents' library. He was well versed in the works of Dickens, Thackery, Shakespeare, Robert Louis Stevenson, and Rudyard Kipling. Occasionally, he would also sneak in a few of Jack London's adventure stories, although Ed Hemingway thought that London's books were too violent to have in the house. And Ernest was an avid reader of a rising Chicago journalist named Ring Lardner, whose articles and satirical stories about baseball satisfied Hemingway's love of sports and his interests in fiction and humor. Ernest soon tried his hand at a few Lardner-like pieces for his school's weekly newspaper, *Trapeze*, and proved to be so

The Oak Park High swimming team (Hemingway is third from left) and foot-
ball team (Hemingway is second from right). Although he loved sports,
Hemingway was a better student than he was an athlete.

successful at that kind of writing that he became an editor
and was generally recognized as the best writer at Oak Park
High. In one of his high school articles, he reported a particularly interesting event in the community involving a student's
act of heroism. Three little girls, he reported, were sitting on
a tottering dumbwaiter when the pulley line snapped and the
girls began their plummet down the shaft. The heroic student

leaned into the shaft and grabbed the line just in time, saving the girls from a certain death. The heroic student in this dubious story was named, of course, Ernest Miller Hemingway.[11] It wouldn't be the last time he used his writing to create a heroic public image for himself.

Ernest was mostly indifferent about *Tabula*, the school's literary magazine. But after the magazine's faculty advisers recognized his talent as a writer, they encouraged him to submit some of his short stories for publication. The three that he finally agreed to submit, "Judgment of Manitou" about Canadian trappers, "A Matter of Colour" about boxing, and "Sepi Jinga" about the Native Americans near Walloon Lake, were certainly immature works given Hemingway's later standards of excellence. But these stories predicted the themes of violence and sporting life that would dominate his later fiction. "Sepi Jinga" in particular, as a story centering on the life of a dog, revealed the influence of Jack London, the writer Ed feared was inappropriate for his upstanding, Protestant household. But Jack London would seem tame next to Ernest's later work, and so it was certain that his later work was not going to appeal to his religious father.

Hemingway and Marcelline graduated on June 13, 1917. (Grace held Marcelline back a year so that she and her "twin" Ernest could begin their schooling together.) Marcelline was a fine student and was selected to read a commencement speech at the graduation ceremony. Ernest was chosen to write and read the class prophesy. The prophesy was a good choice for Ernest because he had already been thinking seriously about the future. Ed expected Ernest to follow the family tradition and join his older sister at Oberlin College in the fall. But Ernest's own plans for himself lay along a very different path. America had just entered the Great War being fought in Europe and all over the world, and Ernest couldn't resist the temptation to join the action. Once again, he wanted to become a "soldser."

Hemingway appears bright and determined in his high school yearbook photo. He graduated from Oak Park High on June 13, 1917.

In August of 1914, nationalist revolutionaries in the European country of Serbia assassinated Archduke Franz Ferdinand, the heir to the Austro-Hungarian empire controlling much of Eastern Europe. The assassination was the final incident in a long series of events threatening the stability of the continent. A century of treaties among European nations, following the defeat of Napoleon in 1815, required that the nations quickly choose sides in the conflict. The Ottomans of Turkey, Austria-Hungary, and Germany made up the Central powers. France, Great Britain, Russia, Japan, and Italy joined to form the Allied powers. World War I began. The United States followed isolationist policies, staying away from the violence in Europe and selling arms and other goods to any nation that offered to buy them. But by 1917, German submarines, or U-boats, had damaged or sunk many American ships, and American businessmen, with more economic interests in the Allied nations than in the Central nations, pressured President Woodrow Wilson to declare war against the Central powers. In particular, Americans feared an aggressive

Germany, a nation seeking conquest and empire. Wilson finally agreed to enter the fray, and on April 6, 1917, Congress approved the declaration of war.

Ed refused to allow Ernest to enlist in the army following the declaration of war. He wanted his son to receive a college education and, more importantly, he wanted to ensure his son's safety. Of course Ernest was upset with Ed's decision, and instead of applying to Oberlin, his father's choice, he applied to the University of Illinois. But he was not happy with the prospect of four more years in the classroom, especially with all of the excitement brewing in Europe. So as a replacement for the excitement he was missing on the battlefields, Ernest thought more and more about the opportunities his writing skills would open for him in journalism and the action he could take part in as a reporter for an inner-city newspaper. Two reporting jobs looked especially promising, one at the *Chicago Tribune* and one at the *Kansas City Star*. Ed's brother Alfred Tyler Hemingway, who lived in Kansas City, was even offering to pass on Ernest's name to his friend Henry Haskell, the *Star's* chief editorial writer, if his nephew was serious about journalism. Ernest accepted the offer and, instead of packing for college, he was set to begin his professional writing career in the fall.

He spent that summer at Lake Walloon, working at Longfield, the forty-acre farm that Grace and Ed had purchased in 1906 across the lake from Windemere. He worked twelve-hour days throughout the summer, helping out at the neighboring Dilworth farm during the slack times in his own schedule. During this period, he also formed close friendships with two young men who would turn up frequently later in his life: Carl Edgar, a twenty-nine-year-old graduate of Princeton, and Bill Smith, a twenty-year-old student from the University of Missouri. Together, they fished, hunted, and worked the farms. And eighteen-year-old Ernest may have even experienced his first romantic interest that summer in

One sport Hemingway enjoyed all his life was fishing. This photo of him was taken at Walloon Lake, Michigan.

Smith's twenty-two-year-old sister Katy. In all, it was an important time for the young adult. Ernest learned how to live an active and independent life away from his parents' constant presence. It was exactly the kind of summer he needed before he moved to Kansas City and scratched out a living for himself in the lonely, urban setting.

Kansas City was a different kind of place from anything Hemingway had known previously. Oak Park had been a well-to-do, relatively safe community. The people of Oak Park were, like Ed Hemingway, deeply religious and averse to many of the diversions for which city life was known. And during Ernest's frequent excursions to nearby Chicago, he had been protected from the seedy underworld and the corrupting influences of city life. But even a modest city like Kansas City had its share of violence and alcohol and gambling. And

Hemingway, free to observe both the bad and the good parts of the city, was thrilled by what he now saw. He finally found the action he had been looking for, and even participated from time to time, acquiring a taste for wine and honing his skills as a bar fighter.

On October 15, 1917, Hemingway moved in with his uncle Alfred Tyler, who had gotten him the job with the *Star*. But their relationship was strained from the beginning. Uncle Tyler was vain, and the kind of parental presence that Hemingway was eager to escape. So he quickly moved out of his uncle's house and into Miss Haine's boardinghouse on Warwick Avenue. A few weeks later, he settled into a tiny attic apartment on Agnes Street with Carl Edgar, his friend from

A proud Ed Hemingway shakes his son's hand soon after Ernest's graduation from Oak Park High. Rather than attend college, the young Hemingway took a reporting job with the Kansas City Star.

Walloon Lake who was now working for a fuel company in town.

Hemingway's starting salary at the *Star* was fifteen dollars a week, but his experiences as a cub reporter were invaluable for his future work as a novelist. The *Star's* style manual described 110 guidelines for the art of writing a good news article. Hemingway would later call them "the best rules I ever learned for the business of writing. I've never forgotten them."[12] Rules about using short sentences and vigorous, positive English were especially influential in shaping the fiction style for which Hemingway would be most famous. He would also gather the ideas and subject matter for some of his later works while working for the *Star*. As a mere cub reporter, Hemingway did not get many tough or influential assignments. Most of his pieces were "color" stories about local brawls and bank robberies, interesting or shocking stories that filled space between the big news articles. But Hemingway pursued these minor stories with boundless energy, actually riding on ambulances against his editor's orders when a particularly violent story caught his interest. His beat, which covered a police station, General Hospital, Union Station, and the shabbier sections of the city with nicknames such as the Yellow Front and the Bucket of Blood, provided Hemingway with plenty of exciting and violent stories. In an age of colorful newspaper reporting, Hemingway was adept at capturing the mood of the city's back alleys and operating rooms, as he displayed in the following passage from an article about the death of a street fighter:

> *The surgeon opened the swollen eye-lids. The eyes were turned to the left. "A fracture on the left side of the skull," he said to the attendants who stood about the table. "Well, George, you're not going to finish paying for that home of yours."... It was merely one of the many cases that come to the city dispensary from night to night—and from day to day for that matter; but the night shift, perhaps, has a wider range of the life and death tragedy—and even comedy of the city.*[13]

Hemingway would write articles like this one so furiously, and he was such a poor typist early in his career, that the editors of the *Star* often couldn't read what he had written. But he attacked his job with relentless enthusiasm, until his attention again turned to the Great War.

As more of his peers sailed across the Atlantic Ocean to take part in the European conflict, Hemingway grew restless. During his year in Kansas City, he tried to enlist in the U.S. army against his father's orders but failed his physical because of an eye defect he had had since birth. Characteristically, Hemingway overlooked the horrors of war and felt as if he were being excluded from a winning football team. "I'll make it to Europe some way in spite of this optic," he wrote to Marcelline after his rejection. "I can't let a show like this go on without getting in on it."[14] When the Kansas City National Guard was ordered to join the troops in France, a volunteer unit called the Home Guard was organized among city residents to fill the guard's role in protecting the home front. Hemingway joined the Home Guard in mid-November of 1917 and was soon busy with practice drills and military maneuvers in addition to his reporting job. Then, in early 1918, officials from the Italian Red Cross arrived in Kansas City to recruit men for the Italian ambulance corps. Hemingway, already thirsty for action and deeply influenced by Hugh Walpole's *The Dark Forest*, a romantic novel about ambulance drivers, immediately signed up. This time, however, he had his parents' approval, because he would be providing a service and saving lives instead of fighting a bloody and often senseless war. Grace and Ed had no idea that Ernest's unbridled desire for excitement would bring him directly into the line of fire.

He returned to Oak Park for a few days after enlisting in the Red Cross to say good-bye to his family. Then he traveled north to his beloved Walloon Lake for a few days of fishing. Bill Smith and Carl Edgar joined him on the lake, as did Charles Hopkins and Ted Brumback, two of his companions from the *Star*. All five men were on their way to Italy for the ambulance corps. By May 12, they were on a train headed for New York City, where they would board a steamer to cross the ocean. But before embarking on the second leg of their journey, they took part in a volunteer parade that marched down glamorous Fifth Avenue in Manhattan. Hemingway, marching as the right guard closest to the grand stand, had a clear look at Woodrow Wilson as the president reviewed the troops. Finally, he felt like a "soldser," the rightful heir to his veteran grandfathers Abba Hall and Anson Hemingway. Though Ernest didn't know it at the time, he would be home again in a few months, and some people would even be calling him a war hero.

LIES AND LOVES

CHAPTER III

Krebs found that to be listened to at all he had to lie, and after he had done this twice he, too, had a reaction against the war and against talking about it. A distaste for everything that had happened to him in the war set in because of the lies he had told.

—*Soldier's Home*

"A BIG LIE is more plausible than the truth," Ernest Hemingway said in an interview in 1959. "People who write fiction, if they had not taken it up, might have become very successful liars."[1] At that time, Hemingway had been "taking up" fiction writing for nearly four decades and wore the mantle of a champion. He was arguably the most successful literary figure America had ever seen. He had the most loyal audience, the most money, and some even said he was the most influential writer in world literature since William Shakespeare. But, just as he suggested in 1959, fiction and lying were two sides of the same coin for Ernest Hemingway, and he was a very good liar despite "taking up" fiction. He told so many different stories about himself that searching for the truth in his life is often like searching for a needle in a haystack.

Perhaps the greatest number of conflicting stories surround his war injuries in Italy in 1918, and Hemingway encouraged them all—especially the ones in which he

A natty Ernest Hemingway
before he went off to serve in a
World War I ambulance unit

appeared most heroic. The *Toronto Star* and his hometown newspaper, *Oak Leaves*, both published stories about how Lieutenant Hemingway, their favorite son, had carried several wounded soldiers on his back after his own legs were riddled with bullets and shrapnel. Letters to Grace and Ed Hemingway, written by Ernest's friends, described how the young Red Cross driver managed to save an Italian comrade after he dug himself out of a live burial. And Hemingway joined the storytellers in a letter that Ed read during a church service, writing about his great courage in the line of fire:

> *The Italian I had with me had bled all over my coat and my pants looked like somebody made currant jelly in them and then punched holes to let the pulp out...They thought I was shot thru the chest on account of my bloody coat.*[2]

In truth, Hemingway was seriously wounded. He had 227

pieces of shrapnel in his legs, pieces of which he reportedly saved to make jewelry, and there may or may not have been a bullet lodged in his knee. But it is nearly certain that there was no more than one bullet, although reports often described many more. And with so many wounds, he could not have performed the heroics he later described, even if he had only the shrapnel to contend with.

Hemingway also claimed to have been the first American wounded in Italy during World War I. Whether this too was a lie is uncertain, but the Italian government treated him like a celebrity anyway, decorating him like a seasoned veteran after only a few weeks in combat. He received the Italian Cross of War and the prestigious Silver Medal of Military Valor. The citation for the Silver Medal, though highly complimentary, omitted any discussion of the more fantastic feats that Hemingway claimed to have performed. Its vague simplicity might be the most accurate record of what actually happened during the late hours of June 7 and the early morning of June 8, 1918:

> Gravely wounded by numerous pieces of shrapnel from an enemy shell, with an admirable spirit of brotherhood, before taking care of himself, he rendered generous assistance to the Italian soldiers more seriously wounded by the same explosion and did not allow himself to be carried elsewhere until after they had been evacuated.[3]

Standing alone, without the embellishments that Hemingway encouraged in the press and among his friends and family, this citation describes him as a participant in a major conflict who made great sacrifices and performed honorably. Perhaps it does not represent Hemingway as a war hero in a strict sense. But it certainly represents him as a worthy heir to Anson Hemingway and Abba Hall, the soldiers of his past.

Still, Hemingway was insecure about his war experience. In his later fiction, and especially in the story "In Another Country," he would suggest that he had gotten his medals for political reasons rather than for any real acts of heroism. The Italians, Hemingway would write, were quick to decorate Americans as an incentive to draw the United States to their defense. Hemingway believed that he may have been one of these politically determined heroes.

Whatever the truth may have been about Hemingway's heroism on the night of June 7, he was badly injured and in need of special medical attention in the following months. From the front, he was transported to the American Red Cross Hospital in Milan, an old city of shaded squares and outdoor cafes in northern Italy. The Red Cross hospital, recently converted from an extravagant mansion into a medical facility, was spotless and still smelled of wood varnish. Hemingway was the hospital's first and, for a time, its only patient. Accordingly, he received the fawning care of the American nurses who were eager to begin their work in the war effort. Hemingway was growing up to be a very handsome young man, and he carried himself with an air of confidence. No doubt he was a very charming first assignment for the young nurses. One nurse, Elsie MacDonald, allowed the nineteen-year-old Hemingway to sneak bottles of liquor into his room against the head nurse's orders. Other nurses would also do him special favors. But it was Agnes von Kurowsky who would have the most lasting effect on Hemingway's life.

At twenty-six years of age, von Kurowsky was seven years older than her patient. She was raised in Washington, D.C., But her Polish and German lineage worried American war officials, who questioned her loyalty to the Allied cause and nearly held up her visa, preventing her entrance into the European conflict. But von Kurowsky was a competent worker and had trained to be a nurse at the incredibly busy Bellevue Hospital in Manhattan. As a result, she was so qualified that she was finally accepted by the Red Cross in spite of her lineage and arrived in Italy on June 15, 1918. She may have been engaged to marry a young doctor in New York before leaving

At the San Siro racetrack, near Milan, Italy, Hemingway is accompanied by three nurses, including Agnes von Kurowsky (at Hemingway's right), who later figured in Hemingway's novel A Farewell to Arms.

for the war but, as a flirtatious and attractive young woman with dark brown hair and shocking blue eyes, she was courted by a number of Italian suitors immediately following her arrival. When Hemingway entered the hospital in Milan, she was already involved with a partially blind, handicapped Italian captain named Enrico Serena. Hemingway and Serena became friends, but Hemingway was enamored with von Kurowsky, and bided his time until his friend left Milan so that he too could join the contest for her affections.

For a few weeks, however, Ernest had other things to worry about and could not pursue Agnes as intently as he might have liked. His injuries were serious. The explosion had left his legs mangled, and he feared that he might lose the use of his right leg, even if his doctors did not amputate. But then his luck changed for the better. On August 10, 1918, Dr.

Sammarelli, an Italian physician, performed surgery on Hemingway's right leg, removing more of the shrapnel lodged there since June 7. The incision over Hemingway's right knee and foot took twenty-eight stitches to close, but the operation was a success. Hemingway's leg was saved and would recover much of its flexibility.

Then on August 26, Captain Serena left Milan. Within a week, Ernest began his largely successful advances on Agnes. In her diary entry on the 26th, Agnes wrote of her attraction to her young American suitor:

> *Ernest Hemingway is getting earnest. He was talking last night of what might be if he was 26–28. In some ways—at some times—I wish very much that he was. He is adorable & we are very congenial in every way.*[4]

In the following months, von Kurowsky appears to have reconciled herself to their age differences and after a long and frustrating period of immobility in his hospital bed, Hemingway soon had a companion with whom to explore the streets of Milan. Together, they would go to horse races, restaurants, and some of the more respectable cafés, living a lifestyle that Hemingway would live again in a few years on the streets of Paris.

Like his colleagues in the ambulance corps, some of the officials at the Red Cross hospital distrusted Hemingway for his recklessness, particularly when it came to alcohol. In her diary, Agnes wrote:

> *Poor kid, I am very sorry for him. Everybody seems to be down on him for some reason, and he gets raked over the coals right & left. Some of the heads have an idea he is very wild and he is—in some respects.*[5]

To the hospital staff's dismay, Hemingway spent a good deal of time drinking. And then, as if he needed encouragement,

Bill Horne, his good friend from Section IV, had arrived at the hospital in August with an inflammation of the intestines. Of course, the two men lived a bit of a high life during their convalescence. In addition, Hemingway had been attending the Anglo-American Officers' Club in Milan and moved through circles of veterans renowned for hard living. In fact, Hemingway's behavior during this period was endangering his recovery to such an extent that even the normally complacent von Kurowsky voiced some concerns. But Hemingway went on with his fast-paced life, even spending some time in Stresa in the western Italian Alps during a brief convalescent leave. During his week's stay in this resort town, he rowed on Lake Maggiore and elbowed his way into Stresa's prominent social scene—including a few drinks with Signor Bellia, one of Italy's richest men, and a round of billiards with a ninety-nine-year-old diplomat and nobleman, Count Emanuele

Hemingway enjoys the company of friends in Milan during his convalescence, 1918.

Greppi. Hemingway might have felt better during this period, but he was pressing his luck with his nightly excursions.

Upon returning from Stresa, Ernest's relationship with Agnes intensified until both of the young lovers were making ardent appeals about the strengths of their affections. With the increasing vehemence of his love for Agnes, Ernest also became increasingly possessive and jealous, tendencies that disturbed Agnes a great deal. Still, she was not disturbed enough at this point to break off the relationship. On October 13, Agnes was reassigned to a Red Cross hospital in Florence for a month. It was a break from each other that both seemed to need. Their correspondence over this period was probably the most impassioned of their relationship.

In the same month, the Italian army began its final offensive against the invading Austrians near Bassano and Monte Grappa, once again north of Venice along the Brenta River. Hemingway, sensing the excitement that surrounded this final campaign in northern Italy, raced to the front to be with his friends Ted Brumback from Kansas City and Bill Horne and Howell Jenkins from the Section IV ambulance corps in Schio. The young men considered the renewal of fighting a cause for celebration. They were together again, in the thick of the action once more. Hemingway and Horne were particularly happy to be together, since they had become even closer friends during Horne's brief stay in Milan weeks before. But during their few nights together, Hemingway drank so much alcohol that he contracted jaundice, a painful liver disorder that forced him back to Milan before the end of the Bassano campaign. Back in the Red Cross hospital, without von Kurowsky's companionship for a few more weeks, Hemingway passed the time writing immature short stories about the war. Soon, he would be attacking his fiction with as much energy as he attacked the bottle.

Agnes returned from Florence on November 11, 1918—Armistice Day, the day that World War I ended. From the moment of her return, her relationship with Hemingway elevated to another level, this time with higher stakes. He was now well enough to visit her on the job, rather than waiting to see her for a few spare moments during the workday. Hemingway would follow von Kurowsky like a shadow, helping her with her chores and sneaking in a few private moments, probably to discuss what Hemingway considered the next, logical step in their relationship: marriage. Hemingway had even chosen Bill Horne to be his best man. After ten days in Milan, von Kurowsky was again transferred, this time to a hospital in Treviso. Perhaps this transfer was not as difficult on von Kurowsky as it was on the young writer. Hemingway's enthusiasm for marriage and his aggressive and jealous behavior were probably more than the flirtatious nurse

Ticker tape rains down and ecstatic crowds fill the streets of New York City in celebration of the end of World War I on November 11, 1918.

had expected from her relationship with the younger man. Nevertheless, her letters at this time were encouraging, and she even participated in plans for the wedding. On December 9, Hemingway visited von Kurowsky in Treviso dressed in full military uniform, decorated with the ribbons and medals he had been awarded by the Italian government. It is possible that his outfit and his behavior on this visit convinced Agnes that Hemingway, though charming, was still something of an immature braggart. They met again on December 31, and Hemingway behaved even more poorly. His jealousy and bad temper governed the day. The next day, New Year's Day 1919, Agnes sent another letter, finally ending their relationship for good:

> *Now, Ernie, I'm looking to you to do big things. Don't worry & fret over me & get silly ideas in your imaginative brain, but carry on and you'll get farther than you would if you sat down & thought of me all the time.*[6]

Her advice was sound and necessary. Their relationship had strayed far from her expectations and desires. But Hemingway was devastated. The new year had begun terribly. Although Hemingway would recycle parts of his relationship with von Kurowsky later during the writing of *A Farewell to Arms*, their real-life love affair was over, and it would only be a source of painful memories for years to come.

Whatever his emotional state was, Hemingway's legs were now sufficiently recovered and capable of sustaining a life away from hospital care. He was sent home. He reluctantly boarded the boat *Giuseppe Verdi* and, after a long trip, stepped down in New York Harbor on January 21, 1919. Limping off the boat, once again in full military regalia, he was interviewed on the docks by a *New York Sun* reporter who would add yet another twist to Hemingway's mysterious wounds: "The stretcher bearers [carrying Hemingway] went down under a storm of machine gun bullets, one of which got Hemingway in the shoulder and another in the right leg."[7] A few days later, an article appeared in the *Chicago American* under the headline, "Worst Shot-up Man in U.S. On Way Home."[8] He received a hero's welcome in Oak Park. The Hemingways' son and brother was a minor celebrity. And Hemingway reveled in hard-won fame. He transformed his bedroom into a sort of a museum showcase for the bayonets, pistols, gas masks, maps, and trophies that he smuggled home from the war. Physically, he cut a gallant figure for his hometown. He was a large, handsome young man. And he wore his uniform often and polished his boots every day before he left the house. But no amount of regalia and pomp could cure him of his haunting memories of the war. He had been stricken with insomnia in the Milan hospital, a condition that was probably aggravated by the sudden conclusion of his relationship with von Kurowsky. A hero in the daytime, he would not be able to sleep without a light burning in his bedroom for months following his homecoming. In some respects, he was as battered and disillusioned as the pessimistic veteran Harold Krebs of his later story "Soldier's Home."

Still, Lieutenant Ernest Hemingway was the popular champion of Oak Park in the early months of 1919. Dressed in his uniform, wearing his medals, walking with a cane, carrying the bloody, shrapnel-punctured trousers he had worn on the night of June 7, he was invited to speak at a number of social clubs, churches, and civic institutions about his war experiences. After a few performances, he developed a routine during which he would re-enact the fateful night of June 7 for his audience, embellishing his own story with details of other war stories he had heard during his stay in Milan. Audiences were enraptured. *Trapeze*, the Oak Park High School weekly, printed a song about Hemingway following an assembly at which the young veteran had spoken. His name was actually included in the chorus: "Hemingway, we hail you the victor./

Hemingway, ever winning the game."[9] Chicago Italian Americans held two parties in the Hemingway house on North Kenilworth Avenue in honor of Lieutenant Hemingway, who told them he fought for the Italian army. Both parties were catered by the finest Italian restaurants in Chicago, featured ethnic mandolin music, operatic performances, and wine, which was an unusual commodity in the conservative, "dry" neighborhood of Oak Park. Although Ernest probably enjoyed these parties immensely, and enjoyed the wine in particular, Ed Hemingway had seen enough drunkenness during the second party and never allowed another celebration of its kind in the house. Prohibition had started in January of that year, so besides Ed's religious aversion, it was also illegal to serve alcohol.

In addition to the parties, Italy was still on Ernest's mind for more serious reasons. He continued to receive letters from Agnes for months following his return to the United States and was learning to accept that they would never be married. But then on March 7, Agnes wrote that she was soon to be married to an Italian lieutenant, Domenico Caracciolo, a Neopolitan and an heir to a dukedom. Agnes and Caracciolo would break off the engagement some months later, but the initial announcement had an immediate, serious effect on Ernest. He became feverish and sick after reading the letter and was bedridden for days under his sister Marcelline's care. Even after he recovered, his life was critically altered. He started drinking even more heavily than he had before and, for a time, lost much of his ambition. He scrapped his recent plans to attend the University of Wisconsin and traveled back up to Michigan in July, in an attempt to escape his sorrow by fishing and hunting with Howell Jenkins and some other friends.

That fall, Hemingway stayed in the town of Petosky on Lake Michigan, first at the Dilworth farm and then at Mrs. Eva Potter's boardinghouse on State Street. It was not a terribly eventful time in Hemingway's life, although he did borrow

Bill Smith's typewriter during this period and began his career as a freelance fiction writer. His first stories written in Petosky fell under the rubric, *Crossroads: An Anthology*. They were tales of small-town folk in Michigan following the models of Edgar Lee Master's poetry in *Spoon River Anthology* and Sherwood Anderson's *Winesburg, Ohio*. He also nurtured a few relationships with some of the local Petosky girls at this time, but none of them would displace the hurt he felt at the loss of Agnes.

Finally, it was the war that brought him good luck once again. To make some extra cash during these fruitless months in Michigan, Hemingway agreed to deliver his now-perfected lecture about his war experiences to a meeting of the Ladies Aid Society in the Petosky town library. One of the women in attendance that day, Grace's friend Harriet Connable, was the wife of Ralph Connable, the head of the F. W. Woolworth chain of stores in Canada. Mrs. Connable was impressed with Hemingway's bravery and his gentlemanly presentation and thought he would be a fine example and male companion for her handicapped son Ralph Jr. She offered Hemingway $50 per month and access to her chauffeur if he would agree to move into the family's well-staffed mansion on Lyndhurst Avenue in Toronto, as nineteen-year-old Ralph Jr.'s tutor, while she and her husband vacationed in Palm Beach, Florida. Hemingway accepted the offer and moved to Toronto in January of 1920.

Hemingway got along well with Ralph Jr., although he had very little to do as a tutor because the boy was already far advanced in his studies. The Connables were impressed with their new employee, and Mr. Connable went out of his way to promote Hemingway's career as a writer. He introduced Hemingway to his friend Arthur Donaldson, advertising chief for the *Toronto Star*. Donaldson then introduced him to editor Gregory Clark. And Clark then introduced him to J. Herbert Cranston, chief editor for the *Star Weekly*. Apparently,

A CENTURY OF 'A PAPER FOR THE PEOPLE'

'MISSING' HEMINGWAY

By Ernest M. Hemingway.

JACK Dempsey, a well-built, scowling, hard faced citizen of Utah, is regarded as a superman by several millions of people.

He has been pronounced the greatest fighter of all time, the hardest hitter, and the fastest heavyweight that ever climbed through the ropes. Many people fear for the safety of Georges Carpentier's life, when he shuts himself into the ring with this tremendous primitive force.

Most persons acquainted with things pugilistic believe that Jack Dempsey won the title of heavyweight champion of the world from Jess Willard at Toledo, Ohio, July 4th, 1919. The formal transfer of the crown did take place there — but Jess Willard lost the title in the Baltimore Hotel in Kansas City, Missouri.

Willard's stupid, kindly face, flushed by his efforts to make the best of the last few months before the strict enforcement of the 18th amendment, was one of the landmarks of the Baltimore. Jess Willard hated fighting and he was very fond of drinking. That doesn't make an ideal temperament for a fighter — but Willard never was a fighter at heart.

Picked by fate and Jack Curley, to be the man to defeat the renegade Johnson in a bout that had been in bad odor with every one acquainted with the back-stage workings of championship fighters, Willard became the champion. He defended his title once in a no decision fight against Frank Moran, a mediocre opponent, and then lapsed into more congenial pursuits.

On July 4th, 40 years old, heavy paunched, untrained and sodden and loggy with two years of steady drinking, he went forth with cow-like courage to fight Jack Dempsey for the championship of the world and $150,000 win, lose or draw. In the first round the slim, sun-browned Dempsey slugged him to the canvas seven times. Willard looked dumbly and stupidly up at the tiger-like youth and staggered to his feet to earn his $150,000. At the end of the third round Dempsey was tired from smashing the big bulk and Willard seemed to be recuperating from the beating he had taken. Willard seemed the fresher of the two — Dempsey was hanging on to him and occasionally socking in a tired manner.

Willard's seconds tossed in a towel at the start of the fourth round. Jess believed he had given the fans a run for their admission — and he didn't need the championship any more — he had $150,000.

That is the way Dempsey won the championship of the world. Since then he has fought twice. The first fight was with Billy Miske, a St. Paul light-heavyweight, and a close personal friend of Dempsey. Miske had been under a doc-

The bloody slugging of prize fighters in the ring was nothing to the callous manoeuvring of managers who arranged championship bouts. The writing style of this overlooked Hemingway feature on Jack Dempsey, which ran on the editorial page on June 25, 1921, anticipates the tone of Death in The Afternoon.

The SUPERMAN myth

In January 1920, Hemingway moved to Toronto, Canada, and for a time contributed articles, such as this one on the prizefighter Jack Dempsey, to the Toronto Star Weekly.

Hemingway made a very good impression on Cranston because he was soon writing humorous color pieces for the weekly paper. His articles usually explored some facet of fishing or city life, and his training in Kansas City proved very helpful for his work on this larger paper. Cranston had unusually literary aspirations for his publication. Hemingway, who of course had his own literary pretensions, fit in well with the *Star Weekly's* style. Some of his articles foreshadowed the humorous but ironic tone that would mark some of his best fiction in later years. In one political satire he wrote for the March 13, 1920 issue, Hemingway utilized the staccato dialogue style he would soon perfect to expose Toronto mayor's, Tommy Church, as an attention-grabbing phony:

> *Between the rounds, the mayor stood up and looked over the crowd. "What is he doing—counting the house?" asked the man next to me. "No. He is letting the sport-loving people look at their sport-loving mayor," I said. "Down in front!" shouted the man next to me in a rude voice.*[10]

Hemingway wrote nearly 160 articles over four years for the *Star*, although in the early stages of his career, during the winter of 1920, his job was anything but stable. In March, after the Connables returned from Palm Beach and his job with Ralph Jr. was completed, Hemingway returned to northern Michigan. He was still hoping to land a more permanent job with the Toronto Paper, but he simply could not ignore the allure of the trout-fishing season in the rivers along the Great Lake.

His return to Walloon Lake was anything but the joyous homecoming he had received the previous winter. Hemingway moved into the guest house at Windemere and invited his friend Ted Brumback to join him. Neither young man held a job, and they spent most of their time lounging around the lake, fishing, hiking, and doing other leisure activities. They were seldom around when Grace needed help with household chores and would even refuse to help when close at hand. Hemingway also shocked his mother with his new habit of using the rough language he had learned in the big cities and during the war. Their relationship deteriorated almost daily until late June, when Hemingway and Brumback committed their final outrage. The two young men supervised a late-night excursion with Sunny, Ursula, and some of their friends to Ryan's Point on Lake Walloon. Grace had no idea that her younger daughters were planning such a trip and wouldn't have allowed it had she known. She blamed her foul-mouthed son and his free-loading friend for putting bad ideas into the girls' heads. Hemingway and Brumback were swiftly thrown out of the house and ordered not to return.

Roaming the streets of Petosky and the countryside of northern Michigan, writing short stories and an occasional *Star* article when his pockets were too empty, Hemingway managed to survive until he found a better opportunity in late October. In that month, he met up with Y. K. Smith, older brother of Bill and Katy Smith. Y. K. worked in the blossoming advertising industry and was an enthusiastic patron of the arts. He and his wife Genevieve, or "Doodles," immediately took an interest in Hemingway and invited the aspiring writer to move into their large, luxurious house in Chicago, at 63 East Division Street. Without having to worry about the bare necessities like food and shelter, Hemingway was now free to begin a serious writing career, exhibiting an impressive work ethic and tremendous discipline during his late-night sessions at the typewriter. It was a time for experimentation. Hemingway continued to write articles for the *Star*, but he also tested his ability to write different kinds of fiction, from serious and violent stories that resembled his later work to political satires and light, humorous pieces. To make some extra money, he worked as a sparring partner for neighborhood boxers at Kid Howard's Gym. And he probably even boxed a few rounds on the roof of Y. K.'s house, betting on the outcome and making a few more dollars for himself. As bookish and literary as he was becoming, Hemingway would never be afraid of rough, physical activity.

But the most important event of his life with the Smiths

was his introduction to Hadley Richardson. Hadley was the daughter of James Richardson, an executive in the St. Louis pharmaceutical industry who committed suicide when Hadley was twelve years old, and Florence Wyman Richardson, a pianist and a believer in certain forms of magic and the occult. Hadley was an accomplished concert pianist in her own right and trained for a professional career. She attended Mary Institute, an all-girls high school, with Katy Smith before attending Bryn Mawr College for a year. After her brief stint in college, she fell in with an artistic crowd of Ivy Leaguers and developed very specialized tastes in music, painting, and literature. But early in 1920, she was back in St. Louis, caring for her dying mother. When Florence died, Katy Smith invited Hadley to spend some time at Y. K.'s house to recover from the emotional strain of the previous months. Hadley had been sickly and frail as a child but, by the time

Intelligent, energetic, and artistic, with a wide range of interests, Hadley Richardson seemed the perfect match for Hemingway, who fell in love with her almost instantly.

she met Hemingway at one of Doodles's parties, she was tall and strongly built with auburn hair and beautiful blue eyes. Given his own weak emotional state following his falling-out with Agnes, it did not take Hemingway long to fall in love with her. Still, at twenty-nine years of age, Richardson was eight years older than her energetic suitor.

Richardson provided an interesting contrast to Grace Hemingway, now the two most important women in Hemingway's life. Grace was an assertive, independent, and self-centered woman straddling the threshold between the Victorian era of strict codes for feminine behavior and the more permissive Jazz Age of the 1920s, when women were testing new freedoms in fashion and social activities. Hadley, on the other hand, was a throwback to an earlier era—shunning the bobbed haircuts and cigarettes of 1920s women, called "flappers," in favor of a more traditional lifestyle in which she, as a woman, would support Hemingway's career first and think of herself later. Their relationship advanced quickly, and even when Richardson returned to St. Louis, her letters to Hemingway were filled with love and encouragement. For his part, Hemingway began the relationship in a manner that was becoming a familiar feature of his social life—he lied, telling Richardson that he had had plans to enroll at Princeton College but was thwarted when his mother used his college money to build her own private retreat at Lake Walloon instead. In addition, he claimed once again to have fought with the Italian army at the defeat at Caporetto, which actually preceded his own arrival at the front.[11] But in spite of the lies, their relationship intensified even while they were separated—one in St. Louis and one in Chicago. Hemingway was so intense in his affection and longing that he apparently suffered bouts of mild depression and migraine headaches in Richardson's absence.

Before Christmas of 1921, Hemingway acquired a job that offered him more security than his previous freelance writing jobs, even if he had to compromise his principles to keep it. He was hired by a magazine called *The Cooperative Commonwealth*, which claimed to be the mouthpiece for the Chicago cooperative movement. The cooperative movement was a vestige of a nineteenth-century reform movement seeking to consolidate business interests for the public good. The movement encouraged the organization of labor unions and the introduction of democratic practices in the workplace. But the magazine that Hemingway worked for was a fraud, the creation of a swindler named Harrison Parker who had very little interest in the plight of labor unions, but very much interest in a quick profit. Hemingway was soon the chief writer for the magazine, writing nearly seventy-five percent of its articles and editorials, even though he knew that he was taking part in a scam. Richardson was more than a little concerned about Hemingway's new job, and she warned him frequently in her letters that he might be in more danger than he realized: "Not having your name connected there may save a lot of trouble for your [literary] name."[12] Hemingway stayed on at the *Cooperative*, however, making $50 a week.

But as Hemingway was compromising his literary name during his days with the *Cooperative*, he spent his nights honing his skills as a fiction writer. In addition, he was making advances into the Chicago literary culture. Y. K. Smith was particularly helpful in this respect, introducing his young boarder to his friends Carl Sandburg and Sherwood Anderson, two of the most influential members of Chicago's literary Renaissance. Sandburg was a middle-aged poet who had entered into the American literary scene in 1914 with *Chicago Poems*, a collection of free-verse poems documenting life in the Midwest. Anderson was a one-time businessman who left his paint manufacturing business in Elyria, Ohio to become a serious writer. After two unsuccessful attempts with novels, he wrote *Winesburg, Ohio* in 1919, a collection of short stories that served as a companion to Sandburg's work on the

During the early 1920s, Hemingway met such Chicago literary figures as the populist poet and essayist Carl Sandburg.

American heartland. By 1920, Anderson was a literary celebrity who had traveled to Paris and worked with an assortment of great international writers congregating there after the war. He would soon be responsible for Hemingway's first big break as a fiction writer. And later he would be responsible for the introduction of another great writer into the literary world—William Faulkner.

Hemingway first impressed Anderson and Sandburg with his careful and passionate reading of some poems in *The Rubaiyat of Omar Khayyam*, a skill he had developed during sleepless nights in Kansas City. The young, aspiring writer must have been delighted to befriend such respected and popular craftsmen, and the affable Anderson took a particular interest in Hemingway's development. Neither man greatly influenced Hemingway's literary style or the way he theorized about writing in 1920. He was already quite set in his ideas at this early date, without having published a word of fiction. He would even argue with Anderson publicly about the correct way to write for an audience. Still, when it came time to decide on a career move that would increase his opportunities as a writer, Hemingway listened to Anderson's advice first.

Hemingway's relationship with Richardson was blossoming quickly and so intensely that the couple was soon writing to each other about marriage. In those letters, Hemingway suggested that they move to Italy to make their start. He was growing terribly homesick for the country, the setting of his greatest glory, and thought that its great artistic history would inspire his own work. In addition, he had repeatedly received invitations from his former Red Cross captain, Jim Gamble, to live with him in his Sicilian villa. Of course Richardson would have agreed to anything that might enhance Hemingway's career, and it appeared as if the move to Italy was a certainty. But Sherwood Anderson told Hemingway to

The American novelist and short-story writer William Faulkner. Faulkner's Light in August *and* Sound and the Fury *are among the great American novels of the twentieth century.*

reconsider his plans. In the early 1920s, Anderson said, Paris was the place to be. Nearly 35,000 Americans were leaving for Paris in the years between 1920 and 1927, perhaps to escape the small-town claustrophobia that Anderson and Sandburg were writing about in their Midwest sketches.[13] Gertrude Stein, the innovative American writer and friend to the great European painters of the age, had been in Paris since 1903, holding court among the young American artists seeking the companionship of their peers. American poet Ezra Pound had arrived in 1920, as did the incredibly talented Irish novelist James Joyce. Paris was indeed a hotbed of activity. The young writers were creating new kinds of fiction, honest and brutal, and were using language in revolutionary ways. Anderson suggested that Hemingway get in on the action early. He wrote generous letters introducing Hemingway to Stein, Pound, Sylvia Beach, a book seller and another prominent figure in the expatriate movement, and the American translator and writer Lewis Galantière. The letters touted Hemingway's skills and his immense potential as a writer and friend. Hemingway, of course, knew a great opportunity when he saw one and was not about to miss the chance to prove himself among the world's greatest artists and thinkers in Paris.

On September 3, 1921, Ernest married Hadley in a small, private ceremony in the Methodist Church at Petosky, Michigan. Bill Smith was his best man and Katy Smith, Bill's sister and Hemingway's former girlfriend, was a bridesmaid. All of the men in the ceremony wore white trousers and dark jackets. It was a very rural event with the reception taking place in a cottage on the Dilworth farm where Hemingway once worked. After throwing Hemingway out of the house the previous summer, Ed Hemingway had to be reassured that his son wanted him at the ceremony. But once the initial uneasiness was passed, Hemingway's parents offered the use of Windemere cottage for the newlyweds' honeymoon. The

Hadley Richardson, on her wedding day. She and Ernest Hemingway were married in Petosky, Michigan, on September 3, 1921.

wedding was a success. The honeymoon was a disaster. The couple was holed up in the cottage for most of their stay, as the temperature dropped way below seasonal expectations. Then they both suffered from bad colds and fevers. Hemingway was able to work on his fiction, however, and finished a violent story about a love affair that would later appear under the title "Up in Michigan."

Hadley was the recipient of a significant inheritance after her mother's death and could sustain them both until Hemingway found a steadier source of income. But in the fall, after Hemingway alerted the *Star* about his intentions to move to Paris, he was hired by the paper as a foreign correspondent

The Hemingways celebrate the marriage of Ernest and Hadley. From left, Ed, Leicester, Sunny, Hadley, Ernest, Grace, Carol, and Marcelline.

covering international events. The Hemingways then bought two tickets to Europe, and on December 8, 1921, they set sail on the French liner *Leopoldina*, from New York Harbor.

Hemingway was only 22 years old, but with his trip to Paris he had turned the page on an entire era of his life. He began his adult life with a wife eight years his senior, a job with a major international newspaper, a promising future, the high expectations of a respected segment of the literary community, and a new home in a foreign land. But he was not a man to forget his roots, and he would always look back to the lessons that he had learned in Oak Park, Michigan, Kansas City, Toronto, Chicago, and of course the Italian front, as the most important of his life. By 1921, he was nearly a fully developed writer, with fixed theories on his craft and on the right way to live life—the Hemingway code of courage, strength, and action.

A year later, while still in Paris, Hemingway received a letter that must have seemed an unreasonable reminder of a past he wanted to forget. It was a letter from Agnes von Kurowsky justifying her actions in the winter of 1920, the first time Hemingway had heard from her in years:

> *I always knew it would turn out right in the end, & that you would realize it was the best way, as I'm positive you must believe, now that you have Hadley. Think of what an antique I am at the present writing, and my ghost should simply burst on the spot, leaving only a little smoke that will evaporate.*[14]

As Agnes suggested, Hemingway was certainly very happy with his new wife, and things appeared to be turning out right for him in the early 1920s. But Hadley was a full year older than Agnes was, even more of an "antique," and there were problems looming large on the horizon of the Hemingways' marriage. And Agnes did not realize that unpleasant "smoke" never "evaporated" entirely from Hemingway's life. He would carry the scars of his failed relationship with Agnes forever.

A FEAST OF FRIENDS

CHAPTER IV

And in that poverty, and in that quarter across the street from a Boucherie Chevaline and a wine co-operative he had written the start of all he was to do. There never was another part of Paris that he loved like that.
—*The Snows of Kilimanjaro*

P ARIS WAS AN enormous, cold, awe-inspiring city when the Hemingways arrived in December of 1921. It was a city with a great literary history, home to some of the late nineteenth century's greatest writers—Verlaine, Rimbaud, and Balzac—in addition to its more recent history as a haunt for American and English expatriate writers. In the 1920s, it was inexpensive for foreigners to live in Paris. Consequently, the city was experiencing something of a literary rebirth, as Sherwood Anderson enthusiastically informed Hemingway. Poor writers flocked to its ancient, celebrated streets and to its outdoor cafés, which were still serving cocktails after alcohol had been banned in the United States in 1919. Hemingway arrived on the scene brimming with excitement. He was a young and memorable figure among the jaded, self-absorbed artists in the bars and cafés. One friend remembered him as "a robust, hulking sort of chap, with a clear skin and a healthy, ruddy color, who is probably the slouchiest dresser in the Montparnasse quarter."[1]

Hemingway, outside his Paris apartment. Two months after their wedding, the Hemingways moved to Paris to live among other ambitious artists and writers.

But even though Hemingway looked more like a lumberjack, he worked hard to become a serious writer. He would live in Paris intermittently for the next seven years, the most intellectually charged years of his life.

During their first days in the city, the Hemingways followed Anderson's advice and stayed at the Hôtel Jacob. They were within walking distance of the Rotond and the Dôme, streetside cafés that also served as meeting places for the hundreds of artists flooding the city. They met up with Anderson's friend Lewis Galantière almost immediately.

During the 1920s and 1930s, expatriate writers and artists frequented the cafés of Paris. One such popular café was La Coupole, located in the part of the city known as Montparnasse.

Galantière was working on French translations of Anderson's books at the time and was eager to assist the writer's young friends. After an expensive dinner at Michaud's, Hemingway, Hadley, and Galantière went back to the Hôtel Jacob, where the two men practiced shadow boxing. An overzealous Hemingway accidentally punched Galantière in the face, smashing his glasses.

With Galantière's help, the Hemingways found an inexpensive apartment at 74 rue du Cardinal-Lemoine on the Left Bank. Unfortunately, there was a noisy saloon below the apartment, and Hemingway found it difficult to concentrate on his writing when he worked at home. For the quiet he needed, he rented another room in a nearby hotel and set up his own office. He was very eager to join the list of Paris' great writers and would even lie to stimulate such associations. Perhaps for this reason, he falsely claimed that this new writing room was the same room in which the poet Paul Verlaine had died.

In his letter to Anderson soon after his arrival in Paris, Hemingway described how well he and Hadley had adjusted to their new surroundings. Of course the adjustments included the return of Hemingway's old crutch—alcohol:

> Well here we are. And we sit outside the Dome cafe, opposite the Rotunde that's being redecorated. . .and we drink rum punch, hot, and the [rum] enters into us like the Holy Spirit.[2]

Life in a foreign nation must have been very difficult for the newlywed couple. The language barrier alone would have been enough to discourage a less-adventurous pair. But they were soon adjusted to the new demands of Parisian life, if they were not yet thriving.

Before settling down to a normal routine in their new apartment, the Hemingways took a second honeymoon in Switzerland. They stayed in warm mountain hotels and learned to ski in the Alps, a recreation both Ernest and Hadley would continue throughout their lives. Returning from Switzerland, Hemingway sent out the letters of introduction that Anderson had written for him. The warm letters drew immediate responses from some of the most-influential people in Paris, and Hemingway soon found himself among the cultural elite.

In early February of 1922, he was invited to the famous apartment of Gertrude Stein, at 27 rue de Fleurus. Gertrude Stein was born in Allegheny, Pennsylvania, in 1874. As a child, she lived throughout Europe and in Oakland, California. For a woman living in an age of strict gender divi-

The American expatriate writer and art critic Gertrude Stein was the friend and adviser of many of the great artistic and literary talents of the day, including Hemingway, who met her in February 1922.

sions, she was very well educated. She attended Radcliffe College, a women's school and now a part of Harvard University, and Johns Hopkins University. After graduating from college, she accompanied her brother Leo on an extended excursion to Paris. Leo was an aspiring painter and wanted be near the great painters of the Impressionist and Post-Impressionist schools. After a brief time in the city, neither

Leo nor Gertrude wished to leave. Instead, they successfully entered the social circles of the age's most experimental artists. And they used some of their money to support many of the most important painters in modern history, among them Pablo Picasso and Henri Matisse. By the time Hemingway met Stein, she was fully engaged in her own career as an innovative writer. She was living with her lifelong companion, Alice B. Toklas, and she was still supporting the avant-guarde of world art. The walls of her apartment were covered with the works of Paul Cézanne, Pierre-Auguste Renoir, Pierre Bonnard, Matisse, Picasso, and Juan Gris. And she was the leading figure in her own literary salon, which periodically included Anderson, William Carlos Williams, and the poet Robert McAlmon. Forty-seven years old in February of 1922, Stein was four months younger than Hemingway's own mother. As Hemingway describes in his Paris memoir *A Moveable Feast*, she was an imposing figure, "very big but not tall and was heavily built like a peasant woman…She talked all the time."[3]

Though a prolific writer, Stein's reputation in 1922 was based solely on her collection of short stories entitled *Three Lives* and on her friendships with great artists. Nevertheless, she had very specific ideas about how to write well and enjoyed teaching her theories to anyone who would listen. Hemingway proved to be a responsive pupil. Early on, Stein liked his short, direct poems but thought that his stories, while promising, were problematic because they were too vulgar and violent to publish. But she continued to work with Hemingway, and the young writer was quick to pick up on Stein's use of declarative sentences and repetition in the *Three Lives* stories. Together, they developed a prose style that would mirror the paintings of Cézanne—short sentences imitating the painter's use of short brush strokes. To further the development of this new style, Stein encouraged Hemingway to become an art collector, beginning with the inexpensive paintings of artists his own age and moving into the more famous works as his career advanced. For the rest of his career, Hemingway would look to the visual arts for inspiration and for ideas about what is valuable in art.

Stein was an important early confidante as well as a teacher for Hemingway, and her influence on his life was enormous. But she was soon competing with Ezra Pound, the American poet, for Hemingway's attentions. Hemingway would later credit Pound as being the best teacher of "how to write and how not to write" that he had ever known.[4] Pound was born in 1885 in Idaho, had degrees from the University of Pennsylvania and Hamilton College, and spent some time as a college professor in America. In 1918, he set off for Europe to become a serious poet. A likable character in the English literary community, he befriended the English novelist Ford Madox Ford, the great Irish poet William Butler Yeats, and an Irish novelist who promised to revolutionize the way future generations would think about writing, James Joyce. Meanwhile, his own career as a poet blossomed and he gathered a following of admirers. He surrounded himself with young talent and encouraged everyone who sought his assistance. Months before meeting Hemingway, he was hard at work editing one of the most important literary works of the twentieth century, "The Waste Land," a poem by a young American writer named T. S. Eliot. Hemingway would always remember Pound fondly, even in old age, when he became cynical and critical of his other friends:

> *Ezra was the most generous writer I have ever known and the most dis-*
> *interested. He helped poets, painters, sculptors and prose writers that he*
> *believed in and he would help anyone whether he believed in them or not*
> *if they were in trouble.*[5]

Pound was thirty-six years old when he first invited Hemingway to his apartment—a small flat cluttered with books, papers, Eastern art, sculpture, and portraits. He was an awkward, confused genius with fiery, unruly red hair. At the time, he was hard at work on an ambitious autobiographical poem called "The Cantos." (He worked on the often bloated and muddled "Cantos" for the rest of his life.) Pound believed in Hemingway's talent immediately, and he promoted the young writer's work in the "little magazines," the literary journals of the Paris avant-guard, most notably *The Dial* and *The Little Review*.

By May of 1922, the "little magazines" started to respond to Hemingway's work. A very small periodical, *The Double Dealer*, published a bawdy tale called "A Divine Gesture." And in June, it published "Ultimately," a poem that is indicative of Hemingway's straightforward and ironic poetic style as well as the influence of Gertrude Stein:

> *He tried to spit out the truth;*
> *Dry mouthed at first,*
> *He drooled and slobbered in the end;*
> *Truth dribbling his chin.*[6]

This poem appeared on the same page as a poem by another young, struggling writer in Paris who would become the other great American novelist of the twentieth century, William Faulkner. Soon, on the merits of this early work and at the behest of Pound and Anderson, Hemingway's stories and poems were appearing in all of the major "little magazines" in Paris.

Hemingway was also finding his own niche in the city's great social bustle. He wrote at the Closerie des Lilas café in the mornings, away from the usual haunts of the expatriates. In the afternoons, he drank at the Dingo café on the rue Delambre, where he gossiped with Jimmie Charters, the well-known Cockney bartender. And at night, he ate at the Nègre de Toulouse restaurant, where the waiters set aside his and

Hadley's own red-and-white checked napkins. He also read voraciously, borrowing books from Shakespeare and Company, a combination bookstore and lending library owned by Sylvia Beach. Beach was a pleasant, warm person, a foppish figure in a velvet smoking jacket and a flowing tie. She too was a major figure in the expatriate movement. Her shop became a favorite gathering place for the more noteworthy

The publisher and bookseller Sylvia Beach stands at the entrance of her Paris bookshop, Shakespeare and Company. The shop, which was also a lending library, was a favorite gathering place for many writers and artists of the day.

writers of the age, and she was often generous with her money—funding the publication of James Joyce's explicit books when no one else was willing to take the risk.

In all, the early months were very happy for Hemingway. But, of course, he experienced his share of setbacks. In February of 1922, he received a letter from his childhood friend Bill Smith, ending their friendship for a time. It appears that Smith took exception to Hemingway's new domineering and superior attitude, a change that had occurred slowly since Hemingway returned from the war. After the young writer had a nasty fight with Bill's brother Y. K., Bill Smith decided that he could no longer tolerate their friendship. "The 1922 Edition of [Ernest Miller Hemingway] is so radically different from earlier Editions," Smith wrote, "that I can only hope time will show equal changes in the reverse direction."[7] Hemingway was distraught for months after the breakup of their friendship.

In addition to the problems in his private life, Hemingway was angry that his busy reporting schedule with the *Star* was severely limiting the time he had for his fiction. He was writing feature articles during his early days in Paris, similar to the articles he had written about trout fishing while living in Chicago. In the first few months, he was given the freedom to write the articles he wanted to write. Often he wrote about the expatriates. His Toronto readership was still of a conservative mindset about the group of artists and outsiders congregating in France's greatest city, and Hemingway tailored his articles to meet their expectations. The articles were often scathing parodies, in which he portrayed his friends as actors and fakers, and settled some of the new rivalries he had accumulated during his first months in the city. But when the hard-edged reporting assignments started to roll in from Toronto, he had to abandon his earlier, light-hearted style for a more serious journalistic style. And then the traveling began.

He enjoyed at least some of the life of a foreign correspondent. He would frequently appear at the Anglo-American Press club, where he would share cocktails with some of the most-important journalists of the age and gather some inside information about the complicated political structures of Europe in the postwar era. For the most part, however, the European beat was hard work, and Hemingway had to relearn much of his old craft for the job. His writing style was more appropriate for a future novelist than for a future political journalist. In March of 1922, after his first round of complaints about how newspaper work was detracting from his fiction, Hemingway was sent to the International Economic Conference in Genoa, Italy. The Genoa conference was the first major international summit following the Versailles convention that ended World War I. Between April 10 and May 13, he wrote and cabled twenty-three anecdotal, vivid articles about his observations at the conference. Only twenty-three years old at the time, Hemingway still had much to learn about the political process. As a result, his stories were often more colorful than informative, more entertainment than hard journalism.

After his weeks in Genoa, Hemingway and Hadley went on a number of excursions together to make up for their month-long separation. They went on a forty-mile hike through the forests outside Paris, and a trout-fishing trip on the Rhône River with Chink Dorman-Smith, an English soldier and Hemingway's friend since the war. Then they went to Milan, to the horse races and the old battlefields of Hemingway's memories. (To Hemingway's disappointment, much of northern Italy had been successfully rebuilt in the three years since the war ended.)

In late September, Hemingway was called out of Paris again, this time to cover the Greco-Turkish War, a war over the Middle Eastern land ceded to Greece in the 1919 Treaty of Versailles. It was a terribly bloody war, leveling entire cities. Hemingway was stationed in the hard-hit Constantinople.

Most of the public sanitation facilities in the city were destroyed. As a result, Hemingway contracted malaria. But, however bad the living conditions had been, it was a fruitful trip for Hemingway's later writing career. Hemingway improved his skills as a political observer, and he accumulated material for his future stories and novels. As a witness to the Greek withdrawal from the city of Adrianople, for instance, Hemingway would write an article entitled "A Silent, Ghostly Procession," much of which he would later recycle for the scene of Italian retreat in his 1929 novel *A Farewell to Arms*:

> *It is a silent procession. Nobody even grunts. It is all they can do to keep moving. Their brilliant, peasant costumes are soaked and draggled. Chickens dangle by their feet from the carts.*[8]

Like many moments in Hemingway's mature works, it was a description of the horrors that accompanied war's heroic glories. As Hemingway grew older, he was coming to understand both sides of battle.

In December of 1922, the *Star* called on Hemingway once again to travel to Lausanne, Switzerland, to cover a conference deciding the territorial questions of the Greco-Turkish War. During his stay at Lausanne, Hemingway wrote a long series of articles, illegally selling some to both the *Star* and the *Star's* competitors for international news, the newspapers owned by William Randolph Hearst. He was never caught, however, and probably made a large profit from his double-dealing.

The highlight of his Lausanne work was his second interview with Benito Mussolini, the young prime minister of Italy. Mussolini was the creator of the Fascist Party, which had forcefully risen to power in the fall of 1922, in the wave of dissolution sweeping Italy after World War I. Hemingway's first interview with Mussolini had taken place the previous June. As a young, inexperienced international correspondent,

Hemingway and the renowned American, muckraking journalist Lincoln Steffans at the Lausanne Conference, Switzerland, in 1922.

Hemingway had been immediately taken with Mussolini's strong presence. He wrote:

> *A patriot above all things, [Mussolini] saw what he regarded as the fruits of Italy's victory being swept away from her in 1919 by a wave of communism that covered all of Northern Italy and threatened all private property rights.*[9]

But after his experiences in Genoa, and perhaps after some much-needed journalism lessons from a famous South African newsman named William Bolitho Ryall, Hemingway was a more objective observer in Lausanne. As a result, his second interview with Mussolini portrayed the leader more truthfully as a dangerous revolutionary and a tyrant. In characteristic Hemingway bravado, the young reporter wrote of this second meeting:

Mussolini is the biggest bluff in Europe. If Mussolini would have me taken out and shot tomorrow morning I would still regard him as a bluff. The shooting would be a bluff. Get a hold of a good photo of Signor Mussolini sometime and study it. You will see the weakness in his mouth which forces him to scowl the famous Mussolini scowl.[10]

However far he had matured as a journalist and a political spectator during the Lausanne Conference, Hemingway continued to resent his work and the time it took away from his true love, fiction. In a letter to Hadley, he wrote, "I'm so sick of this—it is so hard. Everybody else has two men or an assistant, and they expect me to cover everything by myself."[11] Hadley took this letter, and others like it, as a very bad sign of Hemingway's mindset. She decided to visit her husband for a few days in the Alps, to lift his spirits with a skiing holiday. In addition, she packed away all of Hemingway's manuscripts and carbon copies, knowing that a surprise reunion with his fiction would do more than she could to cheer him up. Before boarding the train at the Paris station, she handed the suitcase of manuscripts to a porter. But the suitcase never surfaced after the train pulled into Lausanne. Almost all of Hemingway's work from the past two years had been either lost or stolen and no one seemed to know anything about it. The Hemingways continued with their vacation after the terrible loss, skiing in Chamby and in Montreaux with Chink Dorman-Smith. But Hadley's carelessness with the manuscripts placed a terrible strain on their marriage. In fact, their once-happy marriage would never recover. In time, Hemingway would grow resentful of his wife, even though Ezra Pound assured him that the loss of the early works was a valuable break with the past.

In the winter of 1923, the Hemingways took another train to visit Pound at his home in Rapallo in northwest Italy. They went on a number of walking tours through the beautiful countryside in February and March, but the weather was almost always bad, and the young couple suffered from severe boredom. Hemingway did have some good luck in Rapallo, however. During his stay with Pound, he met Edward J. O'Brien, the editor of an annual series of books entitled *Best Short Stories*. Hemingway showed O'Brien one of the two stories to survive the Lausanne train fiasco, "My Old Man." O'Brien was awestruck and promised to include the story in the 1923 edition of the series, though it had never been published before. In addition, Hemingway met Robert McAlmon, an acerbic poet and a friend of Pound and Sylvia Beach. At the time, McAlmon was working hard to promote James Joyce's outlawed novel *Ulysses* and was developing his

The poet, translator, and critic Ezra Pound. The Hemingways visited the author of Cantos *in 1922 at his home in Rapallo, Italy.*

own publishing imprint, Contact Editions. Hemingway was an unknown in 1923. But on the strength of his literary friends and his own self-promotion, McAlmon promised Hemingway that he would publish a collection of his stories and poems for Contact Editions whenever Hemingway felt that he had enough good, new material. Suddenly, Hemingway was on the verge of joining the select group of published writers in Paris, a very small group in spite of the great flocks of writers who continued to flood the city from America.

On February 18, still in Rapallo, Hemingway learned of an even more startling development in his life. Hadley was pregnant. Normally a joyous event in the life of a father, the announcement drew a less-favorable response from Hemingway. He claimed that he was too young and ambitious to have a little mouth to feed, and he still had no steady source of income. As with the loss of the manuscripts, Hadley was the real victim of Hemingway's displeasure. Immediately following the announcement, Hemingway sent a proposal to Toronto for eight to twelve articles about the French postwar occupation of Germany's Ruhr valley. The proposal was accepted. This job would, of course, take him to the Ruhr and away from his now-pregnant wife. But that seemed to be Hemingway's intent all along.

Then, returning from Germany, Hemingway immediately set out to organize a trip to Spain so that he could witness the great springtime festivals of the *corrida*, the bullfights. Gertrude Stein had been an enthusiastic supporter of the bullfights for years and encouraged Hemingway, with his interests in violence and ceremony, to see the traditional Spanish sport for himself. Hemingway approached the *corrida* as a substitute for the glorious action of war:

> *The only place where you could see life and death, i.e. violent death now that the wars were over, was in the bull ring and I wanted very much to go to Spain where I could study it.*[12]

The trip was a huge success. The Hemingways traveled from Madrid to Seville to Ronda and finally to Granada, following the raucous, colorful festivals with great interest. Apparently, it was even a happy time in their marriage, a reprieve from the strained circumstances surrounding the lost manuscripts and the pregnancy. And Hemingway finally decided to make a sacrifice for his young family. He agreed to leave Paris and return to Toronto, where Hadley and their new child could be placed under the care of the more-skilled North American doctors.

Before returning to Toronto, Hemingway finished the proofs and oversaw the development of his first book with McAlmon's Contact Editions, *Three Stories and Ten Poems*. The "ten poems," though the more popular elements of the book in 1923, are basically ignored by modern scholarship. The "three stories," however, are considered classics of the developing Hemingway style. Two of the stories, "Up in Michigan" and "My Old Man," survived the Lausanne catastrophe because they were hidden in Hemingway's desk at his writing apartment. The third, "Out of Season," was written following his recent trips to Italy. In addition to *Three Stories and Ten Poems*, Hemingway was revising his work for a second, slender book for William Bird's Three Mountains Press. This second book, entitled *in our time*, was a series of violent and poetic vignettes, each a few sentences long, about themes as diverse as fishing, war, and the bullfights. Many of the vignettes had been published earlier, in the spring 1923 issue of *The Little Review*. In book form, Hemingway deftly wove these short pieces into a coherent picture of the world following World War I.

Hemingway felt closed in and stifled after returning to Toronto in the fall of 1923. He rented an apartment on Bathurst Street but spent most of his time away from his pregnant wife, working long hours at the *Star*, as a city reporter. The editor of the newspaper disliked Hemingway and gave him only the least-interesting assignments.

Hemingway was outraged. But the editor may not have been entirely at fault. Hemingway was terribly arrogant about his writing ability now that he had spent some time with the masters in Paris and had a published book of his own. (*Three Stories and Ten Poems* was finally printed and distributed in August.) His arrogance made him difficult to work with. But, by ignoring his obvious talents, the editor only angered Hemingway and made him even more difficult to work with. And Hemingway's private life did not make up for his dissatisfaction with his job. He continually complained about his wife's pregnancy, and he felt acutely the constraints of a more-conservative, North American society. While European culture accepted Hemingway and his hard-drinking, hard-living friends, alcohol was still an illegal commodity in the United States, and some of the antialcohol feeling had apparently rubbed off on the Canadians. In a letter to Ezra Pound, Hemingway claimed that his days in Toronto inspired him with a new understanding of Sherwood Anderson, who once abandoned his family and his job to escape the restrictions of small-town American society:

> *I have not had a drink for five days. It makes a man understand Anderson. On my second year here I would have run down the road. It's the only thing for a man to do.*[13]

On October 10, Hadley gave birth to Hemingway's first child, John Hadley Nicanor Hemingway. "John Hadley" was a name under which Hemingway had written many of his first Kansas City and Toronto articles. "Nicanor" was the name of one of Hemingway's new heroes, a bullfighter he had seen in Madrid. "Bumby," as the Hemingways called their son, was a healthy baby with a round, full face and large eyes. Truly a bundle of joy. But even the birth rankled Hemingway, this time because he could not be in Toronto when Hadley went into labor. Instead, he was in New York, against his wishes,

*John Hadley Nicanor
Hemingway, or Bumby,
as Ernest and Hadley
Hemingway called their
son, was born on
October 10, 1924.*

covering the arrival of former British Prime Minister Lloyd George. Now that the life of the journalist did not suit his needs, it was only a matter of time before Hemingway left the *Star* entirely.

That winter, with Hemingway in a constant rage over his reporting job and Hadley nursing their newborn son, Hemingway's second book *in our time* was published. Grace and Ed Hemingway received a number of copies at their home in Oak Park. But the explicit nature of some of the vignettes, particularly those dealing with war and women, was offensive to the writer's religious parents. Ed sent every copy back to Paris. Hemingway was intensely disappointed in his parents' decision and mulled it over for years, finally sending them an explanation of his writing style in 1925, perhaps the best explanation he ever offered:

I'm trying in all my stories to get the feeling of actual life across. . .So that when you have read something by me you actually experience the thing. You can't do this without putting in the bad and the ugly as well as what is beautiful. . .If I write an ugly story that might be hateful to you or to Mother, the next one might be the one that you would like exceedingly.[14]

It was a well-planned explanation, but it did not win his parents' unequivocal support. Grace and Ed would never be truly comfortable with the subject matter of their son's stories.

It is possible that the Paris publication of *in our time* turned Hemingway's head back to the ancient city for good. He resigned from the *Star* on December 23 and left for New York on January 14, 1924, illegally violating the lease on the Bathurst Street apartment. From New York, the Hemingways

The cover of the Paris edition of Hemingway's in our time, *a collection of short vignettes, was published in Paris by Three Mountains Press in 1924.*

boarded the liner *Antonia* and set sail for Europe. This second stay in Paris would begin as the leanest, most-impoverished time in Hemingway's life. All the bad luck seemed to come at the same time. Hadley's investment manager had mismanaged and lost all of the money she had inherited from her deceased uncles and mother. Without the *Star* job, Hemingway could no longer write an article for money when funds were low. A series of his stories were rejected by the "little magazines." And now he had three mouths to feed instead of two.

Hemingway immediately renewed all of his old friendships upon returning to Paris. Stein and Toklas sponsored Bumby's baptism at St. Luke's Episcopal Church, along with Chink Dorman-Smith. Pound was still wandering through the city, working on his *Cantos* and assisting less-fortunate artists. And now Ford Madox Ford, a friend of Pound and

Three of the most important literary figures of the twentieth century—Ford Maddox Ford, James Joyce, and Ezra Pound.

one of the preeminent English novelists of the time, was creating a new magazine, *the transatlantic review*. Though Hemingway and Ford were often at odds about the definition of good literature—with Ford championing an older, Victorian standard—Ford offered Hemingway a job as editor. Hemingway accepted and was soon working for the most influential magazine of the expatriate movement. In its very short run, *the transatlantic review* published nearly all of the important and innovative writers of the 1920s.

Meanwhile, Hemingway continued to labor over his own work. The initial Paris reviews of *Three Stories and Ten Poems* and *in our time* were lukewarm at best. Besides drawing comparisons with the works of Anderson and Stein, they did little to set Hemingway apart as the next great American writer. Hemingway was disappointed with the reviews, and, characteristically, he took his anger out on his friends. Once the comparisons were made in the reviews, Hemingway began to distance himself from Anderson and Stein on artistic as well as on personal levels. Other new friendships were blossoming, however. In the summer of 1924, he met John Dos Passos, the Chicago-born author of *Three Soldiers*, a novel of war and disillusionment that appealed to Hemingway when it was released in 1921. Dos Passos, like Hemingway, had been an ambulance driver in Italy during World War I, although it is doubtful that the two men ever met in 1919. In late June, Dos Passos accompanied Hemingway, Hadley, Chink Dorman-Smith, McAlmon, and others to the San Ferm'n Festival in Pamplona, Spain. Hemingway wanted all of his friends to see the *corrida*. But the trip was not a success. Many people in the group could not stomach the violence of the bullfights. And Hemingway annoyed some people with his insistence that they follow his lead and take part in their own bullfights during the amateur rounds each morning. In addition, he was a dull companion through most of the days, working on a short story that he refused to put down or forget for any length of time.

That story became "Two Big-Hearted River," a true Hemingway classic and the final story in *In Our Time*, his newest book, which would be released in the fall of 1925 by Boni and Liveright publishers. *In Our Time* is Hemingway's most experimental work. It is a series of short stories about life in Michigan and Europe, interspersed with the vignettes from the first *in our time*. Together, the stories and the vignettes combine as an impressionistic document of the young, disillusioned generation that had lost its innocence on the destructive battlefields of World War I. The violence of boxing, bullfighting, and hunting played prominent, metaphorical roles in Hemingway's descriptions, as did alcohol. And *In Our Time* serves as the introduction to the first famous Hemingway hero, Nick Adams. Adams appears in many of the diverse stories—as well as a few later Hemingway stories—and draws the book together thematically. (The Michigan stories also feature a character named "Bill," modeled after Hemingway's estranged friend Bill Smith. Coincidentally, Smith would renew his friendship with Hemingway in December of 1923 after years of silence— without having seen or heard of the book. He would even move into the Hemingways' Paris apartment for a short time in 1925.)

But even with a third book on the way, the Hemingways were strained financially. Ford paid Hemingway very little for his editorial work on the *transatlantic*, and what little they did have was spent on their trips to Spain and Hemingway's visits to the cafés. On some nights, Hemingway would have to go hungry so that Bumby could eat. In order to make a little spare change, Hemingway began hiring himself out as a boxing sparring partner. Then on December 20, the Hemingways vacationed at the Hôtel Taube in Shruns, in the Austrian Alps. Austria was an incredibly inexpensive place to live at the time, and by giving a few skiing lessons and subletting their new

Paris apartment at 113 rue Notre-Dame des Champs, Hemingway even made some money during the trip. Hemingway's willingness to box or ski for money was not surprising to his friends. Most knew him as a very physical man. He certainly was not a typical, bookish literary figure. Often, he was more like a bar fighter. Stories circulated through Parisian society about his willingness to fight his friends' battles for them—especially for James Joyce, who was abrasive enough to start many scuffles but too blind to defend himself[15]—or how he once threatened to punch the editor of a magazine after the editor suggested a different ending for one of his stories.[16] Hemingway prided himself on his physical toughness, and it was this pride that pulled him through the lean times. If he could handle himself so well in bar scuffles, certainly he was tough enough to handle a little hunger until the money started to roll in. Fortunately, he sensed that it would be rolling in very soon.

In February of 1925, Hemingway received a letter from Max Perkins, an editor at Scribner's, a large and well-known Manhattan publishing firm. Impressed by what he had read in *in our time*, Perkins offered Hemingway a contract to write fiction for the larger firm, promising him more money and greater exposure. At the time, Hemingway already had a three-book contract with Boni and Liveright. But he promised Perkins that he would find a way to write for Scribner's in the near future. Perkins made the offer to Hemingway, who was still an unknown in the United States, on the strength of a recommendation by yet another great writer of the era and an early believer in Hemingway's work—F. Scott Fitzgerald. Without having met Hemingway, Fitzgerald was so impressed by the few pieces he had read coming out of Paris that he felt compelled to introduce Hemingway's work to Scribner's, his own publisher.

Francis Scott Key Fitzgerald—a descendent of the writer of "The Star Spangled Banner"—was born in St. Paul,

Minnesota, in 1896, the son of a failing aristocrat. He attended Princeton College and showed great promise as a writer in his days there. His first two novels about the young and wealthy members of American society, *This Side of Paradise* in 1920 and *The Beautiful and the Damned* in 1922, were enormous critical and popular successes. Following his debut in 1920, Fitzgerald was touted as the prince of the Roaring Twenties, the spokesman of the Jazz Age. Around the time he sent Perkins his praise of Hemingway's work, he was finishing his greatest novel and arguably the best novel of the 1920s, *The Great Gatsby*. But even though Fitzgerald had become an enormous success and a celebrity, he was a terribly insecure individual and a heavy drinker, and his admiration for Hemingway soon resembled hero worship. When the two writers finally met in April of 1925, Fitzgerald was drunk

The author of
The Great Gatsby,
F. Scott Fitzgerald, and his wife Zelda, in 1921.

and effusive, and Hemingway immediately thought he was an immature fool. Nevertheless, a friendship did blossom between the two writers that lasted until Fitzgerald's death in 1940. Throughout their relationship, Hemingway played the role of father figure to the older, alcoholic Fitzgerald. It would always be a complicated friendship, and a source of uneasiness to both men, as Fitzgerald remembered:

> [Hemingway] is a great writer. If I didn't think so I wouldn't have tried to kill him that time...I was the champ and when I read his stuff I knew he had something. So I dropped a heavy glass skylight on his head at a drinking party. But you can't kill that guy. He's not human.[17]

There is no evidence that such an event actually did occur. In fact, Fitzgerald seems to have confused a real accident in Hemingway's life with his own actions. But the story is definitely evidence of the tensions between the two writers.

In the summer of 1925, Hemingway returned to Spain with a group of friends, again to Pamplona to see the bullfights. Like the last trip he had organized, this one was not a success either. There were the usual objections among his friends about the violence of the bullfights. And then there were other arguments among the men on the trip. One of the most serious disputes took place over the affections of Duff Twysden, a British aristocrat with bobbed hair and easygoing manners, a liberated, 1920s woman—a "flapper" as one might find in Fitzgerald's novels. This dispute would soon become the basis for Hemingway's novel *The Sun Also Rises*. In spite of the tensions surrounding the vacation, Hemingway had found a new friend in the young, champion bullfighter, Cazetano Ordónez. And he managed to impress some of the Pamplona journalists with his own exploits in the bullring during the morning amateur hours. Soon there would be dubious stories circulating in the United States that Ernest Hemingway, the writer, was also a fearless athlete and a skill-

Hemingway had a love for Spain and a fascination for the bullfights, which provided a backdrop for his 1926 novel The Sun Also Rises, *usually considered Hemingway's best work.*

ful matador. The questionable hero of World War I had returned as a skilled participant in the exotic *corrida*.

After their stay in Pamplona, the Hemingways traveled to Antibes on the French Riviera, to visit their new friends Gerald and Sara Murphy. The Murphys were legends of Europe. With a stable home life and three healthy children, they managed to occupy the center of artistic life along with Gertrude Stein and Ezra Pound, both of whom were slowly fading out of the scene. After Gerald made a fortune in

Manhattan business ventures in the early part of the decade, he left the corporate lifestyle to study painting. Some of his later works drew critical praise. More important than his artwork, however, were the parties that he and his wife threw for the elite of the postwar era: Fitzgerald, Picasso, the poet Archibald MacLeish, and now Hemingway. It was clear by 1925 with their entrance into the Murphy circles that Hemingway and Hadley were moving up through the wealthiest and most-important social cliques in the world of art. The future looked brighter.

And Hemingway was writing a new piece, a novel about his experiences in Spain with Duff Twysden and the rest of his friends. He worked incessantly on the manuscript—2,000 words a day—certain that this was the fiction that would set him apart for good. "I'm turning pro in my next bout," he told a friend, characteristically using boxing jargon to describe his writing career:

> It's an eight-rounder that will put me in the semi-finals. Then when I get into the main bouts and grab those big purses in the States, I'm going to buy me a boat, a house on a tropical island, and go fishing.[18]

Hemingway proved to be a prophet. Just as he predicted, his new book would be a huge success and the money would roll in, he would buy a boat and a mansion on a tropical island, and there was plenty of fishing in his future. But, of course, there would also be enormous complications, some avoidable and some inevitable. Hemingway's life was never easy.

BEST OF TIMES, WORST OF TIMES

CHAPTER V

He knew these two and thought them a handsome young couple. He had seen many handsome couples break up and new couples form that were never so handsome long.

—The Sea Change

*I*N OUR TIME was released on October 5, 1925 to reviews that were truly astounding. Nearly every critic praised Hemingway as a fresh, new voice in world literature. His sharp, declarative sentences, though journalistic in origin, seemed beautifully simple and true in the 1920s, after World War I's horrors had done away with flowery sentiment and inflated poetry. It was now a world of harsh realities, and Hemingway's prose became a model for the literature of the age. In addition, the book's format of loosely related stories and vignettes was a major innovation within a tradition of haphazard short story collections. But even as they heaped praise upon him, the reviewers were often guilty of a major crime in Hemingway's eyes. Once again they were drawing comparisons between Hemingway's new work and the work of his old friends Sherwood Anderson and Gertrude Stein. Hemingway was a proud man and insisted on his own originality. He was also arrogant enough to believe that he was the final judge of good literature.

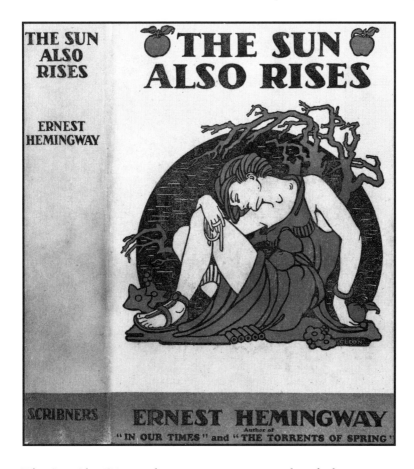

The Sun Also Rises *is the story of two expatriates who embark on an exciting journey from Paris to Spain to see the bullfights, only to discover the emptiness of their lives and the futility of their relationship.*

In his eyes, the comparisons with Stein and Anderson called his own genius into question. As a result, these reviews effectively ended his friendships with both of his true mentors.

While the wonderful reviews of *In Our Time* were pouring in, Hemingway was working on the new novel he had begun after his last trip to Pamplona. This novel would become his first masterpiece, *The Sun Also Rises*. When the rough draft was completed, Hemingway put the book aside for a few weeks so that his mind would be clear before he began the editing process. In the meantime, he began another project, almost entirely for his own enjoyment. This second, more relaxed project, a novella entitled *The Torrents of Spring*, was a humorous parody of the literary world and especially the people with whom he was most often compared. It was his response to the critics of *In Our Time*. In a letter to Ezra Pound, Hemingway wrote, "It is a regular novel only it shows up all the fakes of Anderson, Gertrude, [Sinclair] Lewis, [Willa] Cather ... I don't see how Sherwood will ever be able to write again."[1] He showed the manuscript to many of his writer friends, and everyone agreed that it was perceptive and very funny. Pound and a fawning Fitzgerald even told him to have the book published. But John Dos Passos was more concerned about Hemingway's growing literary reputation and told him to hold off. The book was simply too scathing and would hurt too many people, he said. The main character of *Torrents*, Scripps O'Neil, was a thinly veiled caricature of Anderson, a parody of the writer's personality as well as a criticism of his writing. In the first few chapters, Scripps even abandons his family in a way reminiscent of Anderson's own desertion years earlier. Throughout the book, Hemingway narrates using the trite rhetorical questions that pervaded Anderson's later works, such as *Dark Laughter*:

> *The long black train of Pullman cars passed Scripps as he stood beside the tracks. Who were in those cars? Were they Americans, piling up money while they slept? Were they mothers? Were they fathers? Were there lovers among them? Or were they Europeans, members of a worn-out civilization world-weary from the war? Scripps wondered.*[2]

It was certainly a humorous representation of Anderson's style. But Dos Passos was right to think that it was too harsh to publish against a loyal friend whose only fault was to be compared with Hemingway by the critics.

Nevertheless, Hemingway took Pound's and Fitzgerald's advice and submitted *Torrents* to Boni and Liveright, but for different reasons than anyone suspected. At the time, Hemingway was unhappy that Boni and Liveright had not marketed *In Our Time* more enthusiastically—the great critical success only sold a few thousand copies. And he was also thinking about Max Perkins's offer to accept him into the more powerful Scribner's publishing family. He therefore used *Torrents of Spring* as a pawn in a power struggle. He knew that the book was too bitter and nasty to be accepted by Boni and Liveright, and he also knew that there was a clause in his three-book contract stating that a rejection of his second offering to the publishers would free him from his contractual obligations. Hemingway, therefore, offered *Torrents* as his second book and asked for a $500 advance. When Boni and Liveright rejected the book, as expected, Hemingway was free to shift his loyalties to Scribner's. Hemingway then traveled to New York and received a $1,500 advance from Scribner's, and Perkins agreed to publish *Torrents* immediately. Hemingway was now a major writer who had the additional good fortune of writing for a major publisher.

Hemingway was alone during his brief stay in New York. Hadley and Bumby stayed in Schruns, Austria, where they were vacationing over the winter holidays. It was a difficult time in the Hemingways' marriage. There were major troubles brewing—Hemingway was in love with another woman, and he was wracked with guilt. To escape his problems, he drank too much in between dinner parties with New York socialites and writers, such as Dorothy Parker. But the alcohol provided no relief.

The previous summer, just before the disastrous trip to Pamplona with Hadley and Duff Twysden, Hemingway was introduced to Pauline Pfeiffer, a high school classmate of his childhood friend Katy Smith. Pauline was the daughter of

Paul Pfeiffer, a former commodities broker from St. Louis who had settled on a 60,000-acre estate in Piggot, Arkansas, one afternoon when his train broke down en route to California. Pfeiffer was four years older than Hemingway. She had been a journalism student at the University of Michigan and had worked for the *Cleveland Star*, the *New York Daily Telegraph*, and *Vanity Fair* before settling in Paris with her sister Virginia as a fashion editor for *Vogue* magazine. Originally, Pfeiffer was nothing more than a drinking buddy for Hemingway and a good friend to Hadley, accompanying the family for a short time during their stay in Schruns that winter. But soon Hemingway was entranced by the young journalist, who was considerably closer to him in age than Hadley was. And he was writing Pfeiffer very serious love letters and contemplating the breakup of his marriage:

> *[Hadley] won't admit it but she knows we're the same person—sometimes she has admitted it—but instead of giving her the delay that is practically the only thing left in the world that she wants we railroad her toward divorce and smash ourselves both up at the same time.*[3]

Returning from New York after his meetings with Boni and Liveright and Max Perkins, he stayed three days in Paris, with Pfeiffer, before continuing on to meet his family in Schruns.

While it was a difficult season in Hemingway's personal life, the spring of 1926 saw the completion of his first huge success, *The Sun Also Rises*. He submitted the final manuscript to Perkins on April 24, 1926 and Perkins accepted, with a few misgivings about Hemingway's willingness to criticize his contemporaries in print and his willingness to use vulgarity. But even though he had to fight to retain some of the characters' foul language, Hemingway was later certain that *The Sun Also Rises* was his most moral book, "a tract against promiscuity."[4]

The Sun Also Rises is a *roman à clef*, a gossipy novel whose characters are drawn from real people. The narrator, Jake Barnes, is a wounded World War I veteran like Hemingway who, unlike Hemingway, was so badly wounded that he cannot have physical relationships with women. However, Barnes still manages to fall in love with an English aristocrat named Lady Brett Ashley, modeled after Hemingway's friend Duff Twysden. The rest of the characters are even more closely modeled after Hemingway's acquaintances, including Bill Smith, John Dos Passos, and Ford Madox Ford. The tension of the novel is built around the unfulfilled relationship between Jake and Brett, but the novel takes place in various settings—most important of which are Paris and Pamplona— and manages to cover a host of issues ranging from the peculiarities of expatriate society to the bullfights to the proper techniques of trout fishing. And Hemingway wrote with a critical eye, presenting portraits of his contemporaries that were sometimes as harsh as the work he had done in *Torrents*. Ford was one unsuspecting victim of Hemingway's biting pen as was writer Harold Loeb, the model for the unstable, ineffectual character Robert Cohn. Rumors spread quickly through Paris that Loeb was angry enough about Hemingway's portrayal to issue a death threat against Hemingway. Hemingway swaggered and bragged for a time, daring Loeb to follow through with his alleged threat. Nothing ever came of it.

It was lucky for Hemingway that Loeb and his threat disappeared. He did not need any more enemies or any more tension in his life. His situation at home with Hadley was inhospitable enough. That spring, he and Hadley had taken a tour of the Loire valley in northwestern France. Pfeiffer joined them for a time, and her conflict with Hadley had come to a head. There was a brief confrontation between the two women, but Hadley let it pass, opting to challenge Hemingway on his relationship with Pfeiffer only when they had returned to Paris. Hemingway was evasive under her questioning, and then he escaped to Madrid alone for the summer, to see the bullfights and to write in peace. It turned out to be a very productive escape. Hemingway wrote three solid short stories during this period, "The Killers," "Ten Indians," and "Today Is Friday." Meanwhile, Hadley and Bumby traveled to the French Riviera, to Villa America, the summer house of Gerald and Sara Murphy. The Fitzgeralds were there as were the MacLeishes, but it was not a happy time for Hadley. Bumby contracted whooping cough and was quarantined for weeks. When Hemingway left Madrid to meet his family, they were living in the Fitzgerald's home in Juan-les-Pins, far enough away from Villa America so that the Murphys' children would not be infected with Bumby's sickness. It was a terrible visit. Fitzgerald was drunk most of the time and achingly jealous of Hemingway's achievement in *The Sun Also Rises*. His mere presence was becoming unbearable. And Pfeiffer had stayed on at the Fitzgerald house to take care of Bumby—she was immune to whooping cough—making Hadley very uncomfortable. Finally, Hadley and Ernest had little choice but to announce their separation.

Hemingway's friends were shocked but supportive. Gerald Murphy offered Hemingway the use of his Paris studio apartment at 69 rue Froidevaux, while Hemingway sorted through his messy private life. He decided that there was only one thing to do under the circumstances—pursue Pauline with even greater intensity. Reconciliation with Hadley was both impossible and undesirable, so he searched for a way to start a new married life. Religion was an obstacle in the early weeks of his relationship with Pfeiffer. She was a practicing Catholic and wished that her future husband would share her religious beliefs. She encouraged Hemingway to convert from his Protestant upbringing. Hemingway, who enjoyed the elaborate ceremony of the Roman Catholic Mass, needed little encouragement. He even claimed, perhaps falsely, to have been baptized a Catholic on the battlefield in Italy, when he thought he would die of his wounds and had called a priest.

He would maintain his own form of Catholicism for the rest of his life. "I'm practicing but not a believer," he would say. "Only suckers worry about their souls."[5]

The other obstacle to his union with Pauline was, of course, Hadley. She too had moved out of the apartment at 13 rue Notre-Dame des Champs and found a small apartment of her own down the street from Gertrude Stein and Alice Toklas, at 35 rue de Fleurus. Hemingway helped her move into this apartment, carting her things down the Paris streets in a wheelbarrow and weeping all the way. Then Hadley imposed a single condition on their separation: Hemingway and Pfeiffer would be free to marry each other, and she would grant Hemingway a divorce, if the two lovers could survive a hundred-day separation. Hemingway and Pfeiffer complied. Pfeiffer returned to Piggot, Arkansas, steeped in remorse for betraying her friend. Hemingway was absolutely torn between his love for the two women and even contemplated suicide. But Hadley, seeing how much hardship her single request had caused, withdrew her demand and granted Hemingway the divorce. In the settlement, a penniless Hemingway transferred all of the royalties from *The Sun Also Rises* to Hadley and Bumby. In an uncharacteristically penitent and conciliatory letter, Hemingway acknowledged just how important Hadley had been to his life and his career:

> *Will you please just take [the royalties] as a gift without any protestations or bitterness because it really is your right and due and it would make [me] terribly happy if instead you would be very generous and take it as a gift.*[6]

Later, in his Paris memoir *A Moveable Feast*, Hemingway would look back on his divorce from Hadley as the single, greatest regret of his life: "I wished I had died before I ever loved anyone but her."[7]

If Hemingway had treated Hadley unjustly during his

affair with Pauline, the divorce settlement and the royalties from *The Sun Also Rises* must have been a great financial relief to Hadley. *The Sun Also Rises* was released in the United States on October 22, 1926 and caused a minor sensation. (The book was simultaneously released in Europe under the title *Fiesta*.) The critics were even more enthusiastic about this book than they had been about *In Our Time*. And, for an author's first full-length effort, it was surprisingly successful in the bookstores. By mid-December, it had sold 7,000 copies, and Max Perkins was expecting steady sales into the spring of 1927, prompting second and third printings. The postwar audience latched onto the book for its exciting depiction of their misguided generation. And they even found a title for themselves in one of the books epigraphs, a Gertrude Stein quote, "You are all a lost generation." Hemingway originally intended the quote to parody Stein's presumptions about her own abilities as a social observer, thereby introducing the book's satirical edge. But the readers took the quote seriously, and claimed it as their own. Hemingway was soon recognized throughout the literary world as the spokesman for the "Lost Generation." Apparently the only people who were not encouraged by Hemingway's first major work were his parents. Grace, who was outraged by Hemingway's free use of profane language, even wrote her son a discouraging letter in which she admitted that she was still waiting for him to write something of which she could be proud. "I love you dear and still believe you will do something to live after you," she wrote.[8]

Perhaps Grace's letter would have been more appropriate if she had been writing about *The Torrents of Spring*, which had been released during the summer. *Torrents* was as harshly criticized as *The Sun Also Rises* was praised. Most critics agreed with John Dos Passos that *Torrents* was filled with ingratitude and pettiness toward the very writers who cooperated to give Hemingway his start. In particular, they censured his treatment of Sherwood Anderson as indefensibly cruel, though humorous. Hemingway was enraged by the reaction, but there were few people to comfort him. With *Torrents*, he had in some way alienated most of his literary friends except for Ezra Pound, and Pound was becoming more eccentric with age. So he finally wrote Anderson a letter of explanation, seeking to clear the air between them and perhaps to clear his own conscience:

> *You see I feel that if among ourselves we have to pull our punches, if when a man like yourself who can write very great things writes something that seems to me, (who have never written anything great but am anyway a fellow craftsman) rotten, I ought to tell you so.*[9]

Anderson appears to have taken both *Torrents* and Hemingway's letter in stride. The two writers met in Paris during the winter, and Anderson appeared more upset about his own writer's block than about anything Hemingway had said. And Anderson was having an even more serious problem with his alcohol dependence. In truth, Hemingway's book was rather insignificant at the time, and the unbelievably generous Anderson overlooked most of Hemingway's treachery.

Released now from Hadley's restrictions, Hemingway was free to travel with Pauline Pfeiffer, her sister Virginia, and the MacLeishes, to Gstaad, Switzerland, for some skiing over the Christmas holidays. Gstaad was a more-exclusive resort town than Schruns had been, and Hemingway was now leading a more-glamorous life than he had with Hadley—a lifestyle influenced by his newer friends, the Murphys, the Fitzgeralds, the MacLeishes, and his glamorous new fiancée Pauline. Nevertheless, after signing over to Hadley all of his profits from *The Sun Also Rises*, he was nearly broke. Ernest and Pauline were, therefore, becoming more and more dependent on Pfeiffer's wealthy family for the money to continue their exciting lives, and especially on her favorite uncle Gus, a pharmaceutical baron who wished to encourage Hemingway's career.

In March of 1927, Ernest left Pauline and his friends in Gstaad for a driving tour of Italy with his friend, journalist Guy Hickok. This trip was strategically timed to leave Pfeiffer with all of the responsibilities of finding a new Parisian apartment—at 6 rue Férou—and to arrange for their wedding ceremony. When he returned from Italy, the plans were completed and the wedding was held on May 10, 1927 at the church of St. Honoré-d'Eylan. Hemingway's conversion to Catholicism effectively annulled his marriage to Hadley and freed him for a second marriage under Catholic law. Virginia Pfieffer was the bridesmaid and Archibald MacLeish's wife Ada prepared the luncheon. The couple then honeymooned in the secluded village of Grau-du-Roi on the Rhône River on the southern coast of France. Like his first honeymoon with Hadley, however, this short visit to the idyllic Mediterranean coast was not without incident. Sparking a long series of accidents that would plague him for the next few years, Hemingway cut his foot on a rock and contracted an anthrax infection, which forced him to remain bedridden for weeks even after returning to Paris. (Among the later incidents, he would accidentally pull his bathroom skylight down on his head, creating a gash above his left eye that required nine stitches and left a permanent scar.)

After recovering from his infection that summer, he returned to Pamplona for the annual bullfights and festivals—more bad luck. His favorite matadors were all gored during competition that season and Hemingway himself was less successful in the *corrida* than he had been during the amateur rounds in previous years. And then he fell into debt and had to ask Fitzgerald to lend him $100. Still, he was writing well and expected to publish another book in the near future.

His new stories, "The Killers," "In Another Country," "Fifty Grand," and "Hills Like White Elephants," were solid, deeper explorations of the violent themes he had tackled in *In Our Time*, with a few, glaring differences. They were almost all purely masculine stories that dealt with honor and fear and

Ernest and Pauline Hemingway attend the bullfights in Spain during the late 1920s. The Spanish people recognized Hemingway, who had a great passion for and knowledge of the bullfight, as a true aficianado.

friendship among men. Hemingway admitted that this focus on a masculine world was a conscious decision: "In all of these [stories], almost, the softening feminine influence through training, discipline, death or other causes, [is] absent."[10] So when the new collection was finally released in October of 1927, it is not surprising that Hemingway chose the title *Men Without Women*. Once again the critics praised his taut prose style. But this time the subject matter of the stories was subject to less complimentary scrutiny. Virginia Woolf, the famous novelist who was writing for the *New York Herald Tribune*, even denounced Hemingway's characters as a batch of criminals and degenerate human beings:

> *They are the people one may have seen showing off at some cafe, talking a rapid high-pitched slang; because slang is the speech of the herd.*[11]

Despite the bad reviews, *Men Without Women* still sold more than 7,000 copies, mostly on the strength of Hemingway's growing reputation for writing exciting and beautiful prose and for his new status as the guru of the Lost Generation.

By the winter of 1928, Paris was no longer the literary paradise it had been in the earlier part of the decade. Successful writers who had gone to Paris because they could live there cheaply now had the money to return to the United States. Others gave up the artistic lifestyle entirely and went home to raise families. Gertrude Stein's apartment was quieter now, and Ezra Pound lived almost exclusively in northern Italy. Hemingway was ready to leave now as well. He sought to make a new life for himself with his new bride, a life away from the memories of Hadley. Dos Passos, considering Hemingway's interest in fishing and remembering how he once said he would like to live on a tropical island, suggested that Hemingway visit the island of Key West, the southern-most island of the Florida Keys in the Gulf of Mexico. Hemingway visited the island in the spring of 1928, simply to see Dos Passos's dreamland for himself. Unexpectedly, he would make it his home. In Key West over the next twelve years, he would write three more novels, another series of short stories, his first and only play, and his best nonfiction.

Key West is a tiny island one and one-half miles wide and four and one-half miles long. In the 1930s, before the tourism explosion that would follow in the wake of Hemingway's celebrity, it was the home of New England exiles, often criminals, and Spanish-speaking immigrants, as well as the native-born population known as the "conchs." The local economy was based on the fishing industry and on nearby naval and military installations. The fishermen, criminals, and service men combined to give Key West a reputation as a place of rough excitement and hard living.

When Ernest and Pauline arrived in Key West in the

spring of 1928, it was unbearably hot and humid, and Pauline was five months pregnant. They were not going to stay on the island long, but they had to wait a few days for their new car to arrive, a Model T Ford that Pauline's uncle Gus had purchased for them. While they waited, they slept in a room above the service garage at the Ford dealership. These were obviously not the kind of living conditions that they had grown used to, but during this brief delay they fell in love with Key West's rugged charm and its quaint nautical ambiance. They even decided to prolong their stay and rented a small apartment on Simonton Street, still not expecting to make the island their new home.

Hemingway's ready humor and enthusiasm for life quickly won him a new set of colorful friends. There was Josie Russell, a part-time fisherman and rum smuggler and the owner of Sloppy Joe's, a dark speakeasy on Green Street— Hemingway's favorite bar. Then there was Captain Eddie "Bra" Saunders, the owner of a fishing boat and the man who

Pictured here with their new Model T Ford, Ernest and Pauline relax with Ed and Grace Hemingway in Key West, Florida, in 1928.

would teach Hemingway the secrets of nautical life and deep sea fishing. There was Charles Thompson, the wealthy son of a local business entrepreneur, a fellow fishing enthusiast, and soon one of Hemingway's closest friends. Hemingway suddenly felt very comfortable on the island and with these men, perhaps more comfortable than he had been with the writers and artists in the cafés of Paris.

Hemingway was not in Key West a full month before he coincidentally met his parents on one of the local docks. Grace and Ed had been vacationing in St. Petersburg, Florida, and were in the area checking on some of Ed's Florida real estate investments. This meeting left Hemingway with plenty of cause for concern. Ed was not well physically. He now had diabetes and a heart condition and had not felt well for some time. In addition, the Florida investments were failing and the family was suffering financially. But the most worrisome thing for Hemingway was Ed's frame of mind. Over the past year, he had been suffering from very severe bouts of depression, and Hemingway saw the signs during this chance meeting. Ed's rapid change disturbed him deeply. Still, he was relieved that his parents and his new wife had gotten along well, and he counted his blessings.

When he had arrived in Key West, Hemingway had already written twenty-two chapters of a novel about his childhood home of Oak Park. But the writing was labored and Hemingway grew discouraged. He put aside this project for good then, after a brief attempt to salvage whatever was valuable, and started a new novel about his experiences in World War I. He had something of a new lease on life in 1928, with a new home and a new wife, and he wrote furiously.

But in May, "The Mob" arrived and his work on the new book was put on hold. "The Mob" was the name the locals gave to Hemingway's visiting friends, among them Bill Smith and John Dos Passos. Indeed, with their rowdy, late-night drinking at Sloppy Joe's and wandering the streets of Key West, and their early morning fishing trips when they returned with giant tarpon, "mob" was probably an accurate description. It was on this trip that Dos Passos met his future wife, Bill Smith's sister Katy.

Shortly after "The Mob" left the island, Hemingway and Pauline also left and traveled north to Research Hospital in Kansas City where Pauline, like Hadley, could receive the superior care of northern doctors when she gave birth to her first child. It was probably a fortunate decision. On June 27, Pauline was in labor for eighteen hours until the doctors finally decided to perform a cesarean section. It was a dangerous but successful procedure, and both Pauline and her nine-pound baby boy, Patrick, were in good health. After the birth, Pauline and Hemingway took the baby to the Pfieffer home in Piggot, where Hemingway tried to finish the first draft of his new novel while his wife recuperated. But little Patrick would not cooperate. "If he keeps on yelling," Hemingway wrote during this time, "it's a cinch I won't be able to write and support him."[12] He, therefore, left his wife and child at the end of July and joined his longtime friend Bill Horne on a fishing trip through Wyoming. In the town of Sheridan during that trip, Hemingway succeeded in finishing the first draft of his new novel, *A Farewell to Arms.*

That autumn, on the way back to Key West, Hemingway and Pauline made a short tour of the Northeast, stopping first in Oak Park to see his parents. Ed was worse than he had been earlier in the year. His spirits were lower and his health was failing. But there was very little anyone could do for him, so Hemingway moved on to Massachusetts and visited the MacLeishes. Then he met with Max Perkins in New York. Finally, on November 17, he went to Princeton, New Jersey, to meet Fitzgerald for the annual Princeton/Yale football game. Earlier in the year, he had asked Perkins not to give Fitzgerald his new Key West address. Hemingway thought

Fitzgerald was simply too unpredictable and nasty when he drank, and he was drinking all the time now. Zelda Fitzgerald's mental health had deteriorated over the years to the point where she was almost always in some clinic under a doctor's observations, and her illness had taken its toll on her already fragile husband. But even though Hemingway distrusted Fitzgerald more than ever, he agreed to meet him for the game. It was a bad idea. Fitzgerald was drunk even before they met, and he alternated between offensive behavior and plain foolishness for most of the day. After the game, which Princeton won 10-2, Hemingway agreed to accompany Fitzgerald home to Ellerslie, his new mansion in Delaware. He and Pauline stayed at Ellerslie for one uncomfortable night but left the next morning and raced back to the trains bound for Key West. Still, Hemingway could not seem to get rid of Fitzgerald for good. In truth, they would always be friends, even as they grew leery of one another.

On December 6, Hemingway was once again in New York. This time he was picking up his five-year-old son Bumby, who had sailed from France to be with his father for the Christmas holidays. On the train back to Key West, passing through Trenton, New Jersey, Hemingway received the fearful news he might have been expecting. Ed Hemingway had killed himself.

Ed woke up that morning more depressed than ever. During the previous weeks, he had become a man dominated by fear. He was overprotective of his youngest son Leicester. He was afraid of having a heart attack while he was driving his car. He was concerned about his advancing case of diabetes. And finally, he was simply paranoid. On the morning of the 6th, his fears overcame him. He went into the basement of the North Kenilworth house, burned some of his personal papers and then shot himself in the head with his father's Smith and Wesson revolver, a relic from the Civil War.

When Hemingway heard the news, he did not have

enough money to pay for a train to Oak Park. As a last resort, he wired Fitzgerald asking for $100. Fitzgerald came through with the money, of course, even though Hemingway had recently been avoiding him. Hemingway left his son Bumby in the care of some of the railroad porters who brought the child back to Key West, and then he set out for Chicago. Arriving home, he found his mother in a terrible state of grief. She was particularly concerned about the family's finances without Ed's income. Hemingway, who was also not financially secure at the time, was once again in a position to be the heroic oldest son. He promised to pay Ed's estate taxes and to send the family $100 a month for as long as it would take to reassure Grace of the family's solvency.

Hemingway understood his father's decision to take his own life. He understood that Ed had made a choice and had acted on that choice—that decisiveness, after all, was one of the elements of the honor code Hemingway developed in his fiction. But even if he understood, he did not approve. Later in life, he would remember his father as a coward who was too weak to stand up to his overbearing mother. Indeed, he would even blame his father's suicide on Grace and her nagging demands. (In a few months, when she mailed him the Smith and Wesson his father had used to kill himself, Hemingway angrily threw the gun into a lake.) And he would criticize Ed for his selfishness in leaving his family before they were ready for him to go. "[Suicide is] everybody's right," he would say. "But there's a certain amount of egotism in it and a certain disregard for others."[13] Egotism and a disregard for others had never been Hemingway's major concerns in the past. And, tragically, they would not become his major concerns in the future. In fact, he would forget his own criticism of suicide on a fateful morning in 1961. But during the winter of 1929, he was resentful of his father's act. Prior to the morning of the 6th, it seemed as if his life were falling into place. He was working on a new book, he had a new wife, a new son, and a new home where he felt very comfortable. But now, with Ed's death, he was once again steeped in uncertainty. Things always seemed to happen that way for Ernest Hemingway.

THE MAKING OF
A LEGEND

CHAPTER VI

He drew out the swords from the folds of the muleta and sighted with the same movement and called to the bull, Toro! Toro! and the bull charged and Villalta became one with the bull and then it was over.
                    —In Our Time, Chapter XII

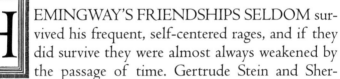EMINGWAY'S FRIENDSHIPS SELDOM survived his frequent, self-centered rages, and if they did survive they were almost always weakened by the passage of time. Gertrude Stein and Sherwood Anderson were now mere names from the past. Hadley too was a memory, still in France and hesitantly engaged to be married once again. Bill Smith had returned after years of silence, but he was less inclined to trust Hemingway as unquestioningly as he had before their falling-out. Even Scott Fitzgerald seemed to be tiring of Hemingway's fatherly advice and his poorly concealed contempt for Zelda. But through all of the petty disagreements and rancor that plagued his other relationships, Hemingway's relationship with his editor, Max Perkins, survived—a testament to Perkins's unbounded patience with the notoriously temperamental writer.

In June of 1929, Hemingway's manuscript for the masterpiece *A Farewell to Arms* was on Perkins's desk. It was the novel that Hemingway had been planning since 1919, both a

Hemingway and his friend the bullfighter Sidney Franklin pose with a giant marlin caught off Key West in August 1934.

story about the Italian ambulance corps during the Great War and a love story about a wounded American driver, Lieutenant Henry, and an English nurse, Catherine Barkley. Hemingway had obviously mined his own experiences with Agnes von

Kurowsky for the novel, but he had skillfully molded that love affair into a tale about the altered state of the world after World War I. The effects were stunning. *A Farewell to Arms* was a tight and exciting adventure story, a romantic tale of ill-fated love, and Hemingway's most-important artistic statement about new literature in the modern world.

In one of the most famous passages in the Hemingway oeuvre, Lieutenant Henry explains the postwar world in terms of the new words one must use to describe it. The passage is a statement about Hemingway's own fiction-writing method as well as a statement about the feelings of his lead character:

> *There were many words that you could not stand to hear and finally only the names of places had dignity...Abstract words such as glory, honor, courage, or hallow were obscene beside the concrete names of villages, the numbers of roads, the names of rivers, the numbers of regiments and the dates.*[1]

Hemingway had been placing a high value on the modest but concrete facts of life since his writing career began. Precise instructions for how to do simple things had always taken up more space in Hemingway's work than the explication of a clear philosophy. Hemingway's readers were always better versed in fishing techniques than in contemporary political or ethical beliefs—although both seemed to infiltrate his best work almost unconsciously. Hemingway was now working to change the way Americans used language. The deadly trench warfare of the Great War had proven that terms like *honor* and *glory* were impossibilities in the modern world—there was nothing glorious or honorable or even civilized about the rodent-infested trenches and the diseases that pervaded World War I battlefields. At least for Hemingway, expertise and the names of things were all that were left.

Perkins was, of course, elated with Hemingway's development as a writer. He knew that he had a best-seller in *A Farewell to Arms*. And Hemingway's new attention to words and their political implications thrilled him. It was Hemingway's attention to other kinds of words, however, that created the tension between the writer and the editor. In previous books, when Hemingway chose to use profanity, the words were hinted at with tricks of spelling and strategically placed dashes. Now Hemingway was demanding that they be written out. Perkins was hesitant to comply. The literary community had never seen the foul words that Hemingway used actually spelled out on the page. Even when Grace and Ed Hemingway had complained about their son's immoral writing, they were referring to obscene words that had been printed with letters missing or replaced with other words so that the reader knew which words were really meant. To print the actual words, Perkins argued, would create an unnecessary sensation. Hemingway disagreed and stood firm in his demands:

> If a word can be printed and is needed in the text it is a weakening to omit it...No one that has read the [manuscript] has been shocked by words. The words do not stand out unless you put a ring around them.[2]

Hemingway had only written one novel at this point in his career and, except for *In Our Time*, his short story collections had only received mixed reviews. One might think that he still had to prove himself as a writer before he could place demands on Perkins and Scribner's. But he was now a minor celebrity of American culture, the voice of the Lost Generation, and the self-proclaimed hero of the battlefield and bullring. And he was so sure of himself and his talent that he refused to back down, especially about a book whose ending he claimed to have rewritten thirty-two times. As one friend remembered, Hemingway's ego was a driving force: "I didn't see how he could get a swell-head [after *A Farewell to Arms*]. He had that, as big as it could stretch, ten years ago. Before he had a dime."[3] Still Perkins won the battle and most of the words appeared in their usual, hyphenated masquerade.

Perkins originally offered Hemingway a $5,000 advance on the magazine rights to *A Farewell to Arms*. But Hemingway was beginning to believe his billing as the most important writer of his generation, and he rejected the offer, holding out until Scribner's changed its offer to $16,000. Accepting that offer, he became the highest-paid writer in the Scribner's family, making even more than the perennial first lady of American letters, Edith Wharton. (In 1933, he would again use his standing as the American literary master to give himself bargaining leverage when Paramount Pictures offered him $5,000 for the rights to make a movie of *A Farewell to Arms* starring Gary Cooper and Helen Hayes. Hemingway held out for $24,000.) Perkins had been correct, however, in believing that the obscene language of the dialogue would obstruct the novel's rise to the top of the American market. In late June, the serial version of *A Farewell to Arms* printed in *Scribner's* magazine was banned from magazine stands in Boston, even though the objectionable words were veiled in the usual manner. It was now certain that even the book version would appear in a hyphenated, censored form. Hemingway lost the war.

The first 31,050 copies of the book were published on September 27, 1929. With the exception of the few critics who consistently complained about Hemingway's use of vulgar language, the reviews were effusive. Dos Passos and Fitzgerald both wrote letters praising their friend and congratulating him on his new title as the heavyweight champion of the literary world. Ford Madox Ford, despite the harsh parody that Hemingway had included in *The Sun Also Rises*, called him one of the "three impeccable writers in English prose that I have come across in fifty years or so of reading."[4] Even Grace Hemingway chose to overlook the book's indecent language and applaud the work as a whole, especially the melodramatic final chapters of the ill-fated Henry/Catherine love affair. Hemingway's only objection to the critics' praises was his old distaste for the comparisons they drew between himself and other writers. In a sarcastic letter to Fitzgerald he wrote:

> Look what tripe everything is—in Plain Talk I learned to write from you—in Town and Country from Joyce—in [The Chicago Tribune] from Gertrude—not yet reported the authorities on Dos Passos, Pound, Homer, McAlmon, Aldous Huxley, and e.e. cummings.[5]

Ernest Hemingway wanted the world to know that he taught himself how to write. He was fully confident now in his own genius. If only the critics could be as confident. . . .

By mid-October of 1929, A Farewell to Arms was closing in on the best-seller lists. Then the Stock Market crashed on October 29, and the executives of Scribner's were afraid that the nation's economic plummet would kill the sale of the novel. But Hemingway's luck was not tied into the luck of his nation. In fact, he seemed to have carved himself a separate existence. The great prosperity of the 1920s, the "roaring" age of jazz and automobiles, had been an unstable prosperity based on appearances more than fact. The rich were buying more than they could afford, relying on credit and running up enormous debts, while the poor and particularly the farmers were losing what little they had. The national economy finally fell to pieces on Wall Street on October 29, when there was no longer enough credit to sustain the "roaring" lifestyle and stock prices fell. Debt overcame the rich, and the Great Depression began. But, while the rest of the country was suffering economically, Hemingway was making money in bundles. And A Farewell to Arms succeeded in reaching the top of the best-seller lists.

In late November of 1929, Hemingway and Pauline traveled to Paris to kick off a year of traveling and adventure. In Paris, they met Fitzgerald and Stein for one last, nostalgic look at the dying salon life at 27 rue de Fleurus. In spite of

Investors panic in the streets following the Stock Market crash of October 1929, the most dire economic downturn in U.S. history.

Hemingway's recent treachery and his unfair public accusations, Stein was a generous host, and gathered the men around her for a lecture about abstract literature and her own prominence in the development of modern prose. Fitzgerald ruined the occasion, however, when he misinterpreted Stein's genuine admiration for his writing as a veiled criticism. In an odd reversal, Hemingway found himself defending Stein's statements to his drunk, insecure, and increasingly unstable friend. On January 10, 1930, Hemingway traveled back to the United States, stopping first in Havana, Cuba, and then in New York City before settling finally in Key West in February, in a house on Pearl Street. It was a strange twist of fate that while Hemingway returned to his masculine paradise at Key West, an impostor was traveling the literary circuits of the northern United States performing at the readings, lectures, book signings, and literary events that Hemingway himself would never agree to attend. Hemingway impostors were only one price of his new-found fame.

In the spring of 1930, in between Caribbean fishing trips with Perkins, Dos Passos, and others, Hemingway wrote a number of short stories and edited a new edition of *In Our Time*. In addition, he began a new nonfiction piece he hoped to expand into a full-length treatise on the art of the bull-fight. During the summer, to escape the humidity and punishing heat of southern Florida, he took Pauline and Patrick to a ranch in the mountains of Wyoming, not far from the trout-filled Yellowstone River. Nordquist Ranch was not a comfortable tourist spot. Instead, it was a working cattle ranch with a large staff of cowboys who provided the legitimate, real-life experiences that Hemingway craved. The cowboys and the burly, wealthy storyteller were soon friends, and Hemingway enjoyed their companionship. He loved Nordquist Ranch so much that he returned almost yearly. In the fall of 1930, Dos Passos joined Hemingway in Wyoming to get in some bear hunting before the season ended. On November 1, the two writers hunted until dark. As they were driving home on a forest road, Hemingway was blinded by the headlights of an oncoming car and drove into a ditch. Dos Passos climbed out of the car unhurt, but Hemingway's right arm was shattered and pinned behind him. After Dos Passos pulled him out of the car, the writers realized the severity of his injury. Hemingway was brought to a hospital for emergency surgery. The doctors cut a nine inch incision in the arm and bound the bones together using kangaroo tendons. The healing process was slow and the arm remained paralyzed for some time, while Hemingway recuperated with Pauline's family in Piggot, Arkansas. He was not a good patient, however, and the inactivity made him restless and even paranoid about his future health.

When he felt good enough to travel, he returned to Key West with Pauline, and the two searched for a new house—this time a permanent residence fitting for a world-renowned author. The house they settled on, at 907 Whitehead Street, did not look like much at first. Though a mansion built in 1851 by a shipping tycoon, it had been uninhabited for years and was a dilapidated and creaking structure when the Hemingways bought it. But they realized its potential. Hemingway, still relying heavily on money from Pauline's Uncle Gus, immediately hired an army of unemployed Key Westerners, the conchs, to begin the renovations. They restored the wrought-iron railings that surrounded the first and second floor verandas, the wine cellar for Hemingway's prize Italian wines, and the carriage house in the backyard, a freestanding structure housing Hemingway's new, second-floor workroom. Under Hemingway's direction, the workroom was connected to the second floor of the main house by a wrought-iron catwalk. Nine hundred seven Whitehead Street became the architectural jewel of the entire island, an impressive home for Key West's most-prominent resident, fully staffed with local domestics, including Dancing Bobby, the butler, and the Prussian governess Ada Stern. The house was completed in 1931, when Pauline was again pregnant and Hemingway was planning a trip to Spain to gather new information for his bullfighting book. (In 1937, Pauline would surprise Hemingway with an addition to the house, the island's first swimming pool, a saltwater basin that also sheltered the family's pet turtle—the favorite animal in the Hemingways' growing menagerie of exotic animals.)

In Madrid and Pamplona during the summer of 1931, Hemingway was once again enthralled by the drama of the *corrida*, which was always a perfect metaphor for his own favorite literary theme—the actions of men confronting death. But, despite his glorious return to the bullfights, Hemingway was disheartened to observe a less-encouraging aspect of modern Spanish culture, the recent outcropping of revolutionaries and radicals among the nation's poor. Once a people who avoided the messiness of politics in everyday life, the Spanish peasants were beginning to realize the disparity between the rich and the poor in their own nation, a disparity magnified by the global economic depression beginning in the late 1920s. Communist dogma was spreading like wildfire through the Spanish countryside, foreshadowing the first major conflict in Europe following World War I, the Spanish Civil War. And with Mussolini on the rise in Italy and Hitler's Nazi Party making a name for itself in economically ravaged Germany, and both countries threatening the delicate balance of European peace, Hemingway was terribly concerned about the fate of his beloved Spain.

After returning from Spain in the fall, Hemingway witnessed the birth of his third son, Gregory Hancock Hemingway, on November 2, 1931. Gregory was a healthy, black-haired, nine-pound child, but his birth caused Pauline a variety of complications. Her labor lasted for twelve hours with the doctors finally deciding to perform a dangerous cesarean section when her life was in danger. Since Gregory's older brother Patrick had also been born by cesarean section, the doctors applied the conventional wisdom of the age and warned Pauline not to have another child. Pauline knew that Hemingway still wanted a daughter, however, so her new physical handicap became a source of great insecurity and discouragement to her. It is possible that she even took some of her discouragement out on little Gregory, whom she usually left to the care of Ada Stern. Nevertheless, Gregory did manage to build a close relationship with his father, remembering only a single instance in his life when the writer raised his voice. "Will you please be quiet!" Hemingway yelled. "I'm trying to write."[6] It was a familiar request in the lives of all of his children.

Hemingway finished his bullfighting book in 1931 and submitted it to Max Perkins, along with a number of photographs of the *corrida* from his private collection. He called the book *Death in the Afternoon*, so when the edited manuscript was returned to him for his approval it was marked "Hemingway's Death." Hemingway railed at Perkins for his insensitivity: "You know I am superstitious and it is a hell of a damn dirty business to stare at ["Hemingway's Death"] a thousand times."[7] Nevertheless, the book moved through Scribner's without a hitch and appeared in the book stores on September 23, 1932. The descriptions of the bullfights, and of the festival culture that surrounds the *corrida*, were by all accounts original and superb. Hemingway had to overcome an American prejudice against the bloody Spanish festivals, and he handled the task masterfully, presenting each contest as a pageant against death and each matador as a hero in an epic struggle. What was less successful in the critics' eyes were the randomly scattered literary anecdotes he included in the middle of his bullfight discussions. The book was filled with parodies such as those that appeared in *The Sun Also Rises*, and even more blatant attempts to justify his own theories about art and literature. Hemingway himself agreed with his critics, even the hated H. L. Mencken, when he admitted to inflating the book with "philosophy and telling the boys."[8]

What he could not agree with, however, was the second most prominent type of criticism his new book received. The critics were now saying that Hemingway's machismo was getting the better of him and clouding his literary judgment. Certainly *Death in the Afternoon* contributed to the picture of a masculine world that Hemingway had begun to compile as early as *In Our Time*. But such critics as Max Eastman now wrote that Hemingway was creating "a veritable school of fiction writers—a literary style, you might say, of wearing false hair on his chest."[9] (In August of 1937, Hemingway would coincidentally meet Eastman in Max Perkins's office. He would tear open his own shirt to display his real chest hair to the critic, and then he would tear open Eastman's shirt to display the critic's own, hairless chest. Then the two men fought in Perkins's office until Perkins and some coworkers managed to separate them.) Gertrude Stein would also engage in the discussion of Hemingway's public persona, concluding that he was a coward and an actor trying to hide his fears. To his loyal readers, however, Hemingway was authentic—a literary adventurer, a living legend and a hero for every hard-living man in America.

Of course, part of the Hemingway myth was fed by the writer's tremendous vitality and enthusiasm for experience. He was a fascinating and magnetic character; some said he was his own most fascinating creation. But another part of the myth was a result of the public's false, romantic notions about his dangerous, self-destructive impulses. In particular, Hemingway and his fans glorified heavy drinking as a socially acceptable pastime, even as they watched alcohol ruining Scott Fitzgerald. In time, Hemingway's own health would suffer from his relationship with the bottle, but by the time he realized his problem, it would be too late to do anything about it. Similarly, Hemingway's self-destructive impulse affected his relationships with women. His fans thought his appetite for women made him even more intriguing. But it had already interfered with his happiness. Certainly Hadley had fallen victim to his wandering eye. And now, in 1932, his relationship with Pauline appeared to be threatened.

On a trip to Havana, Hemingway met twenty-two-year-old Jane Mason, the wife of a Caribbean airline executive and the mother of two adopted children. In many ways, Jane was everything Hemingway disliked about Fitzgerald's wife Zelda. She was beautiful and smart, but she was emotionally unstable and even suicidal. The combination made her a successful manipulator of the men in her life. It is possible that Hemingway knew all of these things and fell in love with her anyway, perhaps hoping that he could rehabilitate her. Whatever he was thinking, Hemingway managed to carry on an affair with the married woman for three years during his frequent fishing trips to Cuba. Pauline was painfully disturbed by the Jane Mason affair. But relief came to the Hemingway marriage when it was most needed in 1932, as Pauline and Ernest began planning for their much-anticipated African safari. The safari would separate the writer from Jane Mason for almost an entire year.

It had always been Hemingway's dream to follow Teddy Roosevelt's footsteps through the African plains, hunting big game. So when Pauline convinced her uncle Gus to underwrite the $25,000 excursion, Hemingway went into training. He visited the famous lion tamer, Clyde Beatty, at a circus in New York's Madison Square Garden, so that he could learn the movements of the great animal he would soon hunt. Then he tried to round up some of The Mob to accompany him on the trip. But most of his friends knew how competitive he was and refused to join. If Hemingway was beaten at his own game and did not come home with the best trophies, they knew he would be even less congenial than the lion he proposed to catch. Only Charles Thompson agreed to make the trip.

The Hemingways and Thompson left for the safari in early August, stopping in Paris and then in Spain along the way. Paris was flooded with refugees escaping the Nazi Party in Germany, and Spain was convulsed in a political crisis that would soon result in civil war. Economic depression had ruined even the most idyllic villages along Hemingway's path, and the bullfights were not as exciting as he had hoped. November 22, the day Hemingway and his fellow hunters were to board the liner *General Metzinger* to cross the Mediterranean to Egypt, could not come too soon. Europe was not the spirited, comfortable place it once had been.

The Hemingways return from an African safari in April 1934. The writer's impressions of the dark continent provide the setting for his 1935 novel Green Hills of Africa.

From the *General Metzinger*, Hemingway mailed a letter to his son Patrick with some of the strangest advice a father ever gave to a five-year-old son, "Go easy on the beer and lay off the hard liquor until I get back."[10] At the time, the letter was probably meant as a joke. But it would not be long before Hemingway's relationship with his sons approached the kind of familiarity he had with his drinking buddies, when the beer and liquor would flow freely between them and the father would be encouraging his sons to be as dependent on alcohol as he was. Gregory was too young to receive a letter in 1933. He was sent to stay with his governess, Ada Stern, in Syracuse, New York. Apparently the Hemingways had no qualms about leaving their youngest child for four months with a strict disciplinarian and a harsh taskmaster. Gregory would later remember Ada as a necessary but frightening presence in his childhood:

Any infraction of her innumerable rules would cause her to fly into a screaming fit...She would pack her bags and go hobbling down the stairs with me clinging to her skirts, screaming, "Ada, don't leave me, please don't leave me!"[11]

However difficult a time Gregory and Patrick were going to have during their parents' absence, Ernest and Pauline did just what two young, glamorous adventurers must do—they left their troubles behind them.

Or at least they tried to leave their troubles behind them. Not long into the trip, Hemingway learned that his third major short story collection, *Winner Take Nothing*, had been published and sold only 12,500 copies. But what was more disturbing than the relatively low number of sales—Hemingway was, after all, a literary hero with a huge following—were the terrible reviews the book received. Following the new trends in Hemingway criticism, the writer was accused of promoting his own heroic persona in such semi-autobiographical stories as "A Natural History of the Dead." Other stories, including "Wine of Wyoming" and "Mother of a Queen," seemed flat and uninteresting when compared with such past masterpieces as "Two Big-Hearted River." After four years of bad reviews following the success of *A Farewell to Arms*, Hemingway once again needed to prove himself to the literary world. But first, there was the hunt.

From the *General Metzinger*, Hemingway and his party continued on to Mombassa, Kenya, where they met up with English master hunter Philip Percival, at his Potha Hill farm. Percival was a World War I veteran who had worked for English intelligence organizations. As if that were not enough to impress Hemingway, whose admiration for soldiers was deep-rooted in the stories of his grandfathers, Percival had also hunted with Teddy Roosevelt, and had the former president's endorsement as an excellent guide through the countryside and a fine hunter of lion. He was handsome, intelligent, and an impressive figure who encouraged his clients and inspired confidence. With Percival's guidance, the Hemingways and Thompson honed their skills by hunting some of the gazelles in the Potha Hill area, and they were soon confident to begin their safari and shoot the real game. They assembled a large convoy for the excursion: two trucks, and a mechanic, a driver, gun bearers, porters, and other hands, all gathered from the native populations.

On the first leg of the safari, Hemingway shot four lions, two leopards, thirty-five hyenas, cheetahs, antelope, eland, and waterbuck. Then misfortune struck while the safari was roaming the Kapiti Plains. Hemingway contracted amebic dysentery, an intestinal disease that caused dehydration and weight loss, and could have been very serious if it went untreated. He had to stop hunting and, grudgingly, waited at the safari camp for two days before a plane arrived to carry him to a frontier station on Lake Victoria in Nairobi. On the way to the station in the plane *Puss Moth*, he was flown past Mount Kilimanjaro, the highest mountain on the African continent. When Hemingway returned to his friends at the camp, he was forty pounds lighter, but he was dazzled by the experiences of this important flight, which he would later explore in his greatest short story, "The Snows of Kilimanjaro."

After his bout of dysentery, Hemingway re-entered the hunt with renewed vigor, landing a rhino, sable, buffalo, zebra, kudu, and oryx during a brief run through the Rift Valley in a country populated by the tribes of the Masai. Also during this second leg of the trip, he visited the Ngong Hills coffee plantation, home to one of his favorite contemporary writers, Isak Dinesen, the author of *Out of Africa*. In all, it was a tremendously exciting time for Hemingway as he traveled a strange and exotic land and successfully hunted game even larger than his marksman father could have imagined. Still, Hemingway could not be entirely satisfied with his trip. First of all, he was leaving too soon. He had come to love the

African plains and its people as he loved Spain and the Spaniards. And, more importantly, he had not won the safari competition that he had created in his mind. Charles Thompson had experienced a spell of beginner's luck and was bringing home larger kudu horns and rhinoceros heads than Hemingway, who was a much better shot. On the boat ride to Europe, Hemingway was troubled by more than a little jealousy.

Back in Paris for a brief time in March before returning home, Hemingway had dinner with James Joyce, his old expatriate friend. But Joyce was morose and drunk for most of the night—yet another confirmation that the glory days of Paris were over. Once again, Hemingway could not wait to leave Europe. On the ocean liner to America, the *Île-de-France*, Hemingway sorted through his Africa experiences and tried to recall the things he would write about when he was back in the States. In addition, he met the famous Hollywood starlet Marlene Dietrich, with whom he would carry on a friendly correspondence for the rest of his life. Perhaps his encounter with Dietrich, a true star of popular culture, was fortunate at this point in his life. Without knowing it, he was just about to attain a level of celebrity few literary men would ever know, before or since.

During the safari, he had written a number of letters for publication in a new men's magazine, *Esquire*. These letters presented his adventures to a broad public, extending Hemingway's persona as a writer and a man of action into homes that had not even known his name previously. After the articles appeared, the Hemingway name began to appear in the gossip pages of popular newspapers along with the other glowing celebrities of the age, including Dietrich. So when he stepped off of the *Île-de-France* after a half year of traveling, society reporters for every major newspaper in the country were waiting for him on the docks, hoping for an exciting anecdote or a good quote from America's favorite man of letters. (Fitzgerald, America's other favorite literary son, had not finished a major novel in nearly a decade.)

Hemingway was now everything he had worked to become—a major writer, a hero of masculine pursuits, and now a national icon. But he saw at an early date that his celebrity status could interfere with his privacy—a writer's most important commodity—so he took precautions. Still in New York after the safari, he visited a shipyard in Brooklyn and commissioned the construction of a thirty-eight-foot cabin cruiser, a fishing boat he could use for deep-sea adventure as well as a means to escape the demands of fame. With a 500-mile cruising range, Hemingway was sure that the new boat, *Pilar*, would help to put some space between himself and his growing number of fans. On *Pilar*, he would read and edit his works, sometimes for weeks at a time. In addition, he would pursue his love for fishing and devise some new, aggressive techniques to make the sport more interesting. Some fishing experts even credit him with permanently changing the character of sport fishing:

> *He initiated the aggressive type of fishing, no doubt about it. . . .Before that tuna had been destroyed by sharks [once they were caught on the fishing line]. Hemingway kept the sharks at bay with machine gun bullets.*[12]

Soon, *Pilar* and its wealthy, daring captain were known throughout the eastern Caribbean. Hemingway's mate, Carlos Gutierrez, only needed to shout "El Hemingway! El Hemingway!" at Cuban patrol boats and the normally hostile troopers would respectfully let the boat pass.[13] And at Bimini, a group of small islands in the straits between Florida and the Bahamas, a frequent stop on the *Pilar* fishing trips, Hemingway was known as Mr. Ernest, the man who promised to box against any challenger in an attempt to stir up the islands' economy.[14]

His Key West home looked more and more like a museum every year, as he accumulated memorabilia from his travels. Now it was filled with trophies from the hunt—hanging skins, horns and antlers, and particularly impressive stuffed heads. In this setting, Hemingway finally set to work on a book about his safari experiences. As in *Death in the Afternoon*, he avoided fictional accounts and wrote what he would later call an "attempt to write an absolutely true book to see whether the shape of a country and the pattern of a month's action could, if truly presented, compete with a work of the imagination."[15] The result was *Green Hills of Africa*, which he worked on in between fishing trips in 1934 and which was published in October of 1935. *Green Hills* was a combination of many different genres. It was a hunter's account of his own exploits, a travel log, a sociological study of native African cultures, and, as always, an artistic statement including Hemingway's own evaluations of the literary world—with predictable asides about Sherwood Anderson's loss of talent and Gertrude Stein's failures. Some critics called it the greatest safari book ever written and praised Hemingway's skillful union of the book's diverse elements. Others thought it was Hemingway's most blatant piece of self-glorification to date. And Edmund Wilson, usually a proponent of Hemingway's work, finally objected to Hemingway's constant criticisms of his contemporaries. "[Hemingway] went all the way to Africa to hunt," Wilson wrote. "And then when he found a rhinoceros, it turned out to be Gertrude Stein."[16]

The criticisms began to affect Hemingway more severely than he ever expected. He wondered what had happened to his talent, and to his firm grasp of the American reading public. He was finally getting a taste of failure. Then, to make matters worse, Jane Mason ended their relationship after four years of secret liaisons. By February of 1936, Hemingway was sinking into the depths of a dangerous depression. He even contemplated suicide for a time. He tried to cheer himself up with more fishing, but that failed. Then he tried to fight himself back to health. One night, he heard that a visitor to Key West, the American poet Wallace Stevens, had called him a coward during a party. Hemingway had never met Stevens before but he went straight to the party and dragged the drunken poet into the street, pounding him with his fists. The fight had proved that he was not a coward, but he was still not cured of his depression.

Then, still in February of 1936, the first installments of Fitzgerald's confessional series of three articles, "The Crack-Up," appeared in *Esquire*. In these articles, Fitzgerald described his own depression, his problems with alcohol, his wasted talent, and the simultaneous "crack-ups" of many of his literary friends. He was penitent now and sincerely regretted wasting his abilities. His writings seemed like a warning to all of his friends who were still traveling along the road of extravagant living, which led to his own demise as well as the total incapacitation of his wife Zelda. It might have been the most mature public statement that Fitzgerald had ever made, and Hemingway should have taken "The Crack-Up" to heart. Certainly his own life was approaching a dangerously fast pace, and his drinking had become a more severe problem in recent years. In addition, his own depression and the mental collapse of his friend Dos Passos were becoming more extreme. But instead of heeding Fitzgerald's sound advice about preserving talent, Hemingway criticized Fitzgerald's masterpiece of honest self-evaluation as a misuse of his prodigious talents. Instead of whining, Hemingway said, Fitzgerald should have concentrated on real literature. Unfortunately, Hemingway considered his own "crack-up" as a symptom of very different problems. He would never trust Fitzgerald's judgment, even though it was better than his own at this point in his life.

Only writing well cured him of his depression. And if Hemingway had ever written well before, he was certainly writing well during the winter of 1936. The two stories to come out of this period, "The Short Happy Life of Francis Macomber" and "The Snows of Kilimanjaro," are by far the best he ever wrote. Both deal with marital discord against the setting of an African safari. In "The Short Happy Life of Francis Macomber," the title character must gather the courage to hunt down a wounded buffalo. Thematically, it is the same courage he must gather to confront his abusive wife. In "The Snows of Kilimanjaro," the lead character is a writer who accidentally cuts his foot during the hunt and is dying from the spread of infection. He too must confront his failed marriage as he prepares himself for death and regrets the stories he would never be able to write—autobiographical episodes from Hemingway's own life. The writing in both stories is tight and sharply poetic, rivaling anything he had ever written, and the plot lines are full of drama and excitement. Once again Hemingway had worked himself into top shape, and he had avoided a mental collapse in the process.

In the spring, a revived Hemingway sailed to Cuba to meet Dos Passos and perhaps bring him out on *Pilar* for some fishing. But Dos Passos was emerging from a dark time in his own life and was hard at work on the book that would save his reputation, a novel dealing with the economic collapse of the previous decade and a future best-seller, *The Big Money*. Hemingway fished alone. However, Dos Passos was able to do one thing for Hemingway during this visit—he forced Hemingway to think seriously about the politics of the modern world. Of course, Hemingway was already painfully aware of the global depression and the imminence of another European war. But as Ezra Pound had complained a decade earlier, he still had not addressed political or economic issues directly in his writing. Hemingway often defended his apolitical outlook in his letters, claiming only to write about loftier themes:

A writer is like a Gypsy. He can be class conscious only if his talent is limited. If he has enough talent all classes are his province. He takes them all and what he gives is everybody's property.[17]

But with the Great Depression threatening the livelihood of his many friends in Key West, and social upheaval threatening to permanently alter the countryside of his beloved Spain, he could no longer hope to be above such issues. He was, therefore, preparing a new novel to deal with the economic issues of the age. And, although he still did not know it, he was about to go back to the battlefield. Hemingway was about to discover just how much influence a living legend can have in world politics.

THE BULLFIGHTER'S CRUSADE

CHAPTER VII

"There were three animals altogether," he explained. "There were two goats and a cat and then there were four pairs of pigeons."
"And you had to leave them?" I asked.
"Yes. Because of the artillery. The captain told me to go because of the artillery."

—**Old Man at the Bridge**

O N SEPTEMBER 2, 1935, a violent and destructive hurricane swept through the Florida Keys. Hemingway's family and property escaped harm, but Hemingway was one of the lucky ones. For the conchs of Key West, the storm could not have come at a worse time. The Great Depression, now approaching its sixth year, showed few signs of letting up, and unemployed laborers throughout the country were utterly discouraged. Even President Franklin Roosevelt's ambitious plan for rehabilitating the national economy, the New Deal, was insufficient to stave off the national decline. America's economic troubles were simply too massive for any plan. Hemingway had always distrusted the New Deal programs. They gave the federal government more influence on the everyday lives of Americans citizens, but as Hemingway noted, the New Deal also brought the dark world of politics directly into American households. So when the hurricane of 1935 hit southern Florida, and destroyed the tent camp of a New Deal agency stationed in

Hemingway spent the late 1930s working as a journalist covering the Spanish Civil War and supporting the Loyalists in their struggle against the Fascists.

the Keys, Hemingway was quick to respond with criticism directed against the Roosevelt administration.

The New Deal agency in the Keys, the Civilian Conservation Corps (CCC), was formed by the Roosevelt administration to create public works jobs for America's unemployed workers. In 1935, the CCC was constructing the first highway to connect the Florida mainland with Key West. Unfortunately, CCC officials failed to heed the warnings of weather experts during the late days of August and did not evacuate as the hurricane approached. When the hurricane blew in and the incredibly strong winds tore through a flimsy tent camp, home to hundreds of war veterans who were hired to build the highway, the CCC had a tragedy on its hands. A day later, when Hemingway went down to the camps to observe the damage, he saw scores of bodies floating in the Gulf of Mexico. Hundreds of workers were killed during the storm.

At the time, Hemingway was living comfortably in his house on Whitehead Street, with his large staff of domestics and his quiet workroom, a retreat from the demands of reality. Nevertheless, he had seen the Great Depression at work. On his drives across the country from Florida to Wyoming, he would often pick up hitchhikers leaving the Dust Bowl of failed Midwestern farms—home to the "Okies" of John Steinbeck's novel *The Grapes of Wrath*. Their stories troubled him deeply, and he was losing his faith in America's promise as the land of opportunity. Now, after the catastrophe of the Florida hurricane, Hemingway decided to speak out against the government, claiming that it was not doing enough for its citizens. For the September 17 issue of *New Masses*, a Communist journal that had not been kind to Hemingway's writing in the past, Hemingway wrote an article entitled "Who Murdered the Vet?" In the article, he blamed Roosevelt and the New Deal for the deaths of the CCC workers in the Keys. They had forgotten the workers, he said, and now the workers were dead. The article was picked up by many of the country's major publications, including *Time* magazine. Soon the whole country was reading about how the famous novelist Ernest Hemingway was accusing the United States government of criminal behavior. "And what's the punishment for manslaughter now?" he had asked.[1]

Simultaneously, Hemingway was working on a novel he hoped would satisfy the requests of his friends Ezra Pound and John Dos Passos, who begged that he enter the political and economic discussions of the era through his fiction. *To Have and Have Not* was the only novel Hemingway would ever write with an American setting. Originally, he had written two separate short stories, "One Trip Across" and "The Tradesman's Return," both about an unemployed fisherman from Key West named Harry Morgan. The editors at Scribner's loved both stories and suggested that he combine them. Hemingway agreed, although he never actually succeeded in creating a unified novel.

In the book, Morgan suffers from the restricted economy of the depression era. His fishing business fails but he still has a family to support. As a result, he accepts a few unscrupulous jobs as a smuggler, carrying liquor from Cuba into America, and Communist revolutionaries from America into Cuba. Both of these jobs end violently, and Morgan is eventually left to die with a single, delirious political message on his lips, "No matter how a man alone ain't got no bloody...chance."[2] The meaning of this line was debated for years after the book was released in 1937. Communists and capitalists both claimed it as an endorsement for their own cause.

But even though *To Have and Have Not* was as politically charged a book as Hemingway would ever write, the ambiguity of this final message was proof that Hemingway would never be an astute political observer, as his friends had hoped. Dos Passos would always have the real political mind, even though Hemingway was the better writer. Hemingway refused to admit to his shortcomings, however, and when he and Dos Passos disagreed about the solutions to the nation's economic crises and the troubles brewing in Europe, Hemingway attributed Dos Passos's differing outlook to character flaws. In addition to their political disputes, Hemingway was more than a little jealous of Dos Passos's incredible success with his last novel, *The Big Money*, which earned the writer a photograph on the cover of *Time* magazine. So, true to form, Hemingway used *To Have and Have Not* to parody his friend. Dos Passos appears in the character of Richard Gordon, a liberal writer who is bribed by wealthy conservatives to support their own causes. The satire is biting and, coming from his friend Hemingway, it hurt Dos Passos terribly. The characterizations of Dos Passos and Hemingway's ex-lover Jane Mason were so obvious, in fact, that the editors at Scribner's feared lawsuits and demanded that Hemingway include the following disclaimer before the opening chapter:

> *In view of a recent tendency to identify characters in fiction with real people, it seems proper to state that there are no real people in this volume: both the characters and their names are fictitious. If the name of any living person has been used, the use was purely accidental.*[3]

Of course the disclaimer was not entirely true. Hemingway had always drawn his characters from real life. And, in *To Have and Have Not*, the characterizations were so blatantly drawn from life that the conchs in Key West amused themselves for days by searching for each other among the book's pages.   And many of them actually succeeded in finding themselves.

In the end, the book's satirical asides only drew attention away from the drama of Harry Morgan's tragedy. They created some of the choppiness for which the book was most often criticized. But by 1936, Hemingway had begun to focus his attention on new challenges, and he rushed to complete *To Have and Have Not*, satisfied to leave the book with many of its flaws. (The attack on Dos Passos is only one example of the excess that slipped through his fingers during the hasty editing process.) The resulting novel is, therefore, one of Hemingway's least impressive works, a critical failure at a time when he desperately needed a critical success. With *To Have and Have Not*, Hemingway could only claim two positive outcomes. First, he had finally won the language war. The actual obscenities he had always written into his dialogue were finally spelled out on the page. And second, in *To Have and Have Not* he had created the vehicle for another Hollywood success, the first movie starring the famous cinematic duo Humphrey Bogart and Lauren Bacall, produced in 1944. The movie was only a success, however, after the book was skillfully adapted for the screen by Hemingway's new rival for the world literary title—William Faulkner.

In January of 1936, Hemingway was hired by *Esquire* to write an article about Benito Mussolini's recent invasion of Ethiopia. Hemingway had been a harsh critic of Mussolini since his early reporting days in Paris, and now he had a chance to smash the Italian leader in a nationally recognized magazine. And he did just that. His article described horrific violence and the atrocities committed by the Italians against the defenseless Ethiopians. It was a vivid piece of reporting. The only problem with the article was that Hemingway had imagined most of the details he described. Writing from his quiet home in Key West, he never accumulated the hard evidence that would have made his article credible. Taking such a short cut, he broke a major rule of journalism—and his own famous rule about writing from experience. No one questioned the authority of Hemingway's article at the time, but his dishonesty in this case must have weighed heavy on his mind. Real trouble was starting again in Europe in 1936, and Hemingway did not want to sit back and write fake articles when he could be experiencing the action firsthand.

As always, Hemingway did not need to be impatient long, the action sought him out later in the year. In July, civil war finally erupted in Spain. Fascist rebels under General Francisco Franco, with the support of Mussolini and Hitler, attacked the strongholds of the Republican government in Madrid, which drew its support from the Communists and other left-wing political groups. The home of the festivals and the *corrida* was now in danger. Hemingway's heroes, the bullfighters, became soldiers and were now fighting against friends from neighboring villages. Communism was still a new economic system in 1936, and Joseph Stalin, the premier of the Soviet Union, was still a hero among the American intellectuals who supported the Communist Party as the party of the workers and the poor. With Stalin's support, the Loyalists of the Spanish government stood up to the invading Fascists and their considerable military strength. The Loyalists also drew some support from Great Britain, France, and, to an even lesser extent, America. But Franco's attacks were overwhelming. A full-scale war had erupted.

By September, John Wheeler of the North American Newspaper Alliance contacted Hemingway—since *Death in the Afternoon*, Hemingway was considered one of the world's leading experts on the bullfight and Spanish culture. Wheeler offered him the job as a syndicated reporter covering the Spanish Civil War for sixty newspapers across the nation, including the *New York Times*, the *Los Angeles Times*, and an occasional column in *Time* magazine. Hemingway was still working on *To Have and Have Not* at Nordquist Ranch when he received the request. He was, of course, emotionally drawn to Spain in its hour of need and lately his life had become too domestic, too patterned and boring to satisfy a man used to constant excitement. The war assignment promised to satisfy both his need for excitement and his desire to assist the Loyalist cause, and he accepted Wheeler's offer.

One problem presented itself before Hemingway was able to get away, however. On a night in December of 1936, Hemingway met a twenty-eight-year-old writer at Sloppy Joe's who had been vacationing with her mother in Key West. Her name was Martha Gellhorn and Hemingway thought she was beautiful. Like Hadley and Pauline, she was from St. Louis. Her father was a gynecologist and a college professor, her mother had been a suffragette like Grace Hemingway. She had attended Bryn Mawr College and had already had a successful journalism career when she met Hemingway, having written for *The New Republic*, the *St. Louis Post-Dispatch*, and *Vogue*. In addition, she had worked with a few New Deal agencies and had befriended the president and Eleanor Roosevelt. Like Hemingway, she had already been divorced once and she was already a great Hemingway fan before they met that first night in Sloppy Joe's. She had even borrowed a quote from *A Farewell to Arms* for the epigraph of her first novel, *What Mad Pursuit*: "Nothing ever happens to the brave." She must have been unspeakably grateful for her chance meeting with the famous writer. But Hemingway was just as excited. Since the Jane Mason affair, his marriage to Pauline had become a series of arguments followed by uncomfortable silences. Gellhorn was young and ambitious and new at a time when Hemingway was looking for something new in his life.

Gellhorn stayed in Key West until January of 1937, weeks after her mother had gone back to St. Louis. She became a friend to Pauline and the two wild Hemingway boys, Gregory and Patrick, before leaving the island for Miami on January 10. Hemingway secretly arranged to meet Gellhorn in Miami and stayed with her until her train left for St. Louis. It was the beginning of the end of his relationship with Pauline. Back in Key West, he quickly prepared for his return to Spain, explaining in a letter to the Pfeiffers that he was leaving his family for the battlefield as a sort of spiritual journey:

> *I hate to go away but you can't preserve your happiness trying to take care of it or putting it away in moth balls and for a long time me and my conscience have both known I had to go to Spain. Can usually treat my conscience pretty rough and even make him like it but it catches up with you once in a while.*[4]

For the first time in his life, Hemingway believed in a cause— the Loyalist cause and the freedom of the Spanish peasants— and he was acting on his beliefs like a noble soldier, a crusader. Of course, he had already convinced Gellhorn to join him in Spain as a reporter for *Collier's* magazine, so he was going to be accompanied on his crusade by a woman who was not his wife. He tried to make up for his infidelity through his enthusiasm for the cause of Spanish liberty. Gellhorn would even admit to falling in love with him precisely because of his newfound loyalty and noble spirit:

> *I think it was the only time in his life when he was not the most important thing there was. He really cared about the Republic and he cared about the war. I believe I never would've gotten hooked otherwise.*[5]

Hemingway was not the only member of the world's literary elite to link his fortune with that of the Loyalist cause. A young English poet named W. H. Auden reportedly enlisted as a stretcher bearer for a brief time in 1937. Novelist George Orwell was to become a lieutenant in the Loyalist army and was severely wounded at the battle of Teurel in 1937. And a group of young, American intellectuals under the leadership of a former university professor, Major Robert Merriman, created a fighting unit called the Abraham Lincoln Brigade. One member of the brigade was the son of Hemingway's childhood literary hero Ring Lardner.

But Hemingway was by far the best-known literary celebrity in Spain in the mid-1930s. And he had the largest pocketbook. He was writing for the extraordinary fee of $500 per wired story and $1,000 per mailed story, and pulling in a considerable profit. Still, Hemingway was a true believer in the Loyalist cause and no mere mercenary. He donated $3,000 of his own money to the besieged government's purchase of ambulances. The Loyalists showed their gratitude by appointing Hemingway the figurehead of the ambulance committee of the American Friends of Spanish Democracy. He also joined an organization of American intellectuals working for the Loyalists, the Contemporary Historians, organizing propaganda in print and film for distribution to the American public. The Historians included playwright Lillian Hellman, Archibald MacLeish, Dorothy Parker, and John Dos Passos. Although some of the Historians supported Communist theories about the enforced, equal distribution of property and some even supported Joseph Stalin, Hemingway distrusted both communism and Stalin. In truth, Hemingway only supported the Loyalists because of his firm belief that it was the party of the common Spanish peasants, the people he had come to love.

Hemingway finally arrived in Spain in March of 1937. Although he was no longer the excitable teenager he had been the last time he was this close to combat, in the summer of 1919, he was still thrilled by the action. He made agreements with the commanders of the Loyalist forces so that he could arrive even closer to the line of fire. His early newspaper reports were filled with examples of his own courage in the face of enemy fire. This time, however, fellow soldiers and journalists agreed with his self-assessment. Even the famous

Hemingway cavorts with Loyalist troops. Although Hemingway's commitment to the Loyalist cause was commendable, his articles and field reports were one-sided.

newspaperman George Seldes was amazed by Hemingway's heroics:

> *As for physical courage, I tell you his daily or almost daily visits to the wrecked building in no man's land he used as an observation post were an exhibition of courage. [Hemingway] and Herbert Matthews climbed out into no man's land almost every day and lay on their stomachs on the floor near a smashed second-floor window to watch the fighting. And Franco shelled everything, including this hideout.*[6]

Hemingway did not only ask this courage of himself, however. He was equally demanding with the friends around him. On March 27, without receiving the official permission required to bring civilians into the war zone, he called upon his friend Sydney Franklin, a former bullfighter born and raised in Brooklyn, and Franklin rushed to join him. Madrid had been under siege for a year, and Franklin had to smuggle himself into Spain according Hemingway's instructions, crossing some of the territory in underground passages behind enemy lines. Even on this perilous journey, Franklin did not forget the coffee and canned goods that Hemingway had ordered. And he did not forget to bring Gellhorn, who set up her own base of operations in the luxurious Hotel Florida in a room next to Hemingway's. Even during the siege, this Madrid hotel maintained a certain level of comfort for its patrons that one could not find anywhere else in the city.

Hemingway's articles from Spain were usually ordinary pieces of propaganda that presented the Loyalist and Soviet party line to the American public. One did not need to know Hemingway to know that he supported the standing government against the Fascist rebels. His articles made his loyalties clear enough. But his friends in the Loyalist effort were all the more grateful for his articles because they were one-sided. As one member of the Lincoln Brigade remembered:

Hemingway was very helpful to the cause of Spain, probably more so than any other prominent public figure. He also wanted to be more in the fight than it was possible for a correspondent to be. He probably gave the impression of being part of the fighting. Many of the Spaniards cooperated with him; they loved him and he had an easy access to leading Spanish commanders and political figures.[7]

Hemingway was in Spain for eight extended visits during 1937 and 1938. In that time, he learned all of the important techniques for survival during wartime. He knew the ins and outs of the black market and could acquire even the most-scarce goods in the war-torn country—like meat and liquor—though few people ever found out where he got them. He was also a good source for classified information. Somehow, Hemingway knew personally almost every general, commander, and politician involved in the war. And he would recount some of what he learned each night during his dinners with his fellow newsmen at Chicote's restaurant—which was little more than a bombed out shell in these years. But his tendency to get caught up in the intricacies of the Loyalist cause sometimes affected his journalism. For instance, he never reported the horrific massacre at Guernica, when German planes strafed the peaceful village with bombs and machine-gun fire, introducing the new danger of aerial assault into modern warfare. The attack was so destructive, and so many innocent lives were lost, that it inspired Pablo Picasso, Hemingway's friend from the Paris days, to create one of his most important and innovative paintings *Guernica*. But the sixty newspapers that Hemingway wrote for never heard of the atrocities. Hemingway was probably somewhere else at the time, helping a Loyalist commander plan his next attack, or trying to find a way to get beef into the besieged city.

On June 4, 1937, Hemingway was invited to speak about the Spanish Civil War at the Second Writer's Congress in New York City. After a silent screening of *The Spanish Earth*, the documentary he had been working on with the Contemporary

Loyalist troops use antiaircraft guns from the trenches as Fascist bombers fly overhead. Despite the courage and perserverance of the Loyalist forces, they were unable to quell the Fascist onslaught.

Historians and director Joris Ivens, Hemingway gave a seven-minute presentation about the state of Spanish affairs. It was a rare public appearance by a man who was surprisingly shy about speaking engagements. But Hemingway realized that the Congress was giving him an opportunity to speak out against what he considered the greatest threat to the modern world, fascism. He spoke passionately:

> *There is only one form of government that cannot produce good writers and that system is fascism. For fascism is a lie told by bullies. A writer who will not lie cannot live and work under fascism.*[8]

When the speech was finished, the audience applauded enthusiastically. But Hemingway left the podium immediately and was too shy to return to the room.

Following this speech, Hemingway stayed in New York

for the Carnegie Hall premier of *The Spanish Earth*, now complete with the narrative that he had written. (World-famous actor Orson Welles was originally hired to read Hemingway's words, but his dramatic style overshadowed the film's visual power. Hemingway wound up doing the final narration in his own, subdued style.) He then went to the White House for a private screening with President Roosevelt and the first lady. Both the Carnegie Hall screening and the White House screening drew positive viewer responses. The film was a success. He then flew to Hollywood for a Contemporary Historians fundraising benefit that eventually raised $20,000 for new ambulances. Scott Fitzgerald was also in Hollywood at that time, under a contract with Metro Goldwyn Mayer studios to write movie scripts, and he attended the Historians' party. Neither he nor Hemingway had any desire to revive their close relationship after so many tumultuous years. Hemingway was now a national icon who had said some very nasty things about Fitzgerald in the past. Fitzgerald was a sad, middle-aged man trying to quit his drinking habit. They parted that night as two old friends who were now doing very different things with their lives. Sadly, it was the last time they would ever be in the same room together.

Hemingway continued to work hard at the propaganda business in July, when he wrote the captions for a pictorial of the war in *Life* magazine. He was now the most important figure in the world for spreading information about the Loyalist cause. When he returned to Madrid in the fall, he was rewarded with access to the tactical and strategic meetings held by the Loyalists' Soviet advisors in Gaylord's Hotel. Still a charming, interesting character, he had reached the inner circles of the unfolding war through his sincere, hard work for the cause.

During this second stay in Madrid, he wrote a play about a Loyalist spy ring in Madrid, *The Fifth Column*, which was loosely based on his experiences with Gellhorn in the Hotel Florida. Published first in 1938 along with his complete collection of short stories to that point, *The Fifth Column and the First Forty-Nine Stories*, the play had a short run on Broadway in 1940 under the direction of Lee Strasburg. Unfortunately it was a flop. Hemingway's distinctive dialogue, so taut and true on the written page, did not hold up under the conditions of the stage. And Hemingway was too possessive an artist to tolerate the collaborative, interpretive style of most theater companies:

> *If you write a play, you have to stick around and fix it up. They always want to fool around with them and make them commercially successful, and you don't like to stick around that long. After I've written, I want to go home and take a shower.*[9]

Around the time he was writing *The Fifth Column*, Hemingway began to separate himself for good from his friend Dos Passos. Following on the heels of *To Have and Have Not*, the collapse of their friendship was the result of political differences. Dos Passos was losing his fervor for the Loyalist cause. An astute observer of international politics, he was slowly realizing that a Spain under the guidance of the Soviet Communists, and particularly under Joseph Stalin, was little better than a Spain controlled by Mussolini. The international community was beginning to realize the extent of Stalin's tyranny during this time, as information about his "purges"—his summary executions of the millions of people he feared as traitors—became public knowledge. Dos Passos himself had recently lost a good friend to Stalin's paranoia. His Spanish translator, José Robles, had disappeared months earlier and was subsequently reported to have been mysteriously murdered. Dos Passos suspected the Communists and when he tried to find out the truth about Robles's death, Hemingway accused him of snooping and threatening the Loyalist cause. He then accused Dos Passos of writing articles about the war in ignorance of the real issues. "When people read a series of articles running over six months or more from you they do not realize how short a time you were in Spain and how little you saw," Hemingway wrote. Then he closed the letter with an insult: "Hope you're always happy. Honest Jack Passos'll knife you three times in the back for fifteen cents and sing Giovenezza free. Thanks pal."10 In retaliation for Dos Passos's alleged treachery, Hemingway wrote propagandizing articles with a renewed fury. And he foolishly entangled himself with the Communists when he wrote an article entitled "The Barbarism of Fascist Interventionists in Spain" in August of 1938 for the Soviet party newspaper Pravda. In the same issue were articles by the American writer Upton Sinclair, author of the muckraking novel The Jungle, and the Chinese Communist revolutionnary, Mao Tse-tung.

By now, Hemingway was going too far in his support of the Loyalists, just as Dos Passos warned. Stalin was not a man to support, even if he was on what Hemingway considered the correct side of the war. But it took a different crisis of international proportions to alert Hemingway to the dangerous game he was now playing with Stalin and the Soviet powers. While the war between fascism and communism was being fought in Spain in 1938, Adolf Hitler was threatening to absorb areas of central Europe. In September, British Prime Minister Neville Chamberlain met with Nazi leaders in the German city of Munich, hoping to coax Hitler out of his aggressions. Returning from the Munich convention, Chamberlain proclaimed the meeting a success. He declared that he had purchased "peace in our time." Britain and its allies agreed to transfer part of Czechoslovakia to Germany with Hitler's assurance that he would end his campaign of European aggression. Hemingway was distrustful of the agreement from the beginning, and knew instinctively that Hitler would go back on his promise at the first opportunity. Suddenly it occurred to him that the Spanish Civil War was a prelude to another, more destructive war to come. Neither the Communists nor the Fascists actually cared about the Spanish people, he realized, as long as they won their strategic positions in Spain. So he was already disillusioned with the war effort by mid-November of 1938, when the Battle of the Ebro ended the war in Spain and Franco became the new dictator of the land.

Hemingway was a changed man when he returned to the United States after the war. As was the case in 1919, he was plagued with nightmares about the battles he had witnessed. But he was also a different kind of person during the waking hours—a man who had experienced failure and large-scale tragedy, who had rubbed elbows with the most important historical figures of the age, a wizened veteran and a man who had secured his own place in history through his propaganda efforts in support of the Loyalists. He was older now, a little heavier around the belly, and his hair was thinning and turning white. And he had a new nickname which seemed to encapsulate all of these new elements to his character—he was now known to the world as Papa.

Martha Gellhorn had accompanied Hemingway through Spain for most of the war. After the Battle of the Ebro, she returned to the Western Hemisphere and rented a house outside Havana, Cuba, on a fifteen-acre plot of land known as Finca Vigìa, or "Lookout Ranch." It was a spacious mansion in a palatial setting complete with a swimming pool, a tennis court, a watchtower, and even a group of ruins in one corner of the land. Hemingway could not stay away from Gellhorn long, and he captained *Pilar* back and forth between Key West and Havana for a time. Meanwhile, his marriage to Pauline collapsed. In the summer of 1939, Pauline had had enough of their bickering and escaped to Europe with her sons. When she left, Hemingway moved in with Gellhorn and fell in love with Cuba. He enjoyed the Havana baseball teams and the café Floridita almost as much as he had enjoyed the conchs and Sloppy Joe's in Key West. And he was working on a new novel about the civil war, which was flowing easily and developing into the greatest story he had ever written. Gellhorn too was working on a new novel, this one about her experiences with Hemingway, *The Stricken Field*. During the summer, he did not return to Nordquist Ranch, his favorite vacation spot since the early 1930s. Instead, he was invited to stay at the brand new resort lodge of Averell Harriman, the director of the Union Pacific Railroad, in Sun Valley, Idaho. Sun Valley was exactly the kind of vacation spot Hemingway had always sought and a good replacement for Nordquist Ranch. He could hunt in the nearby Sawtooth Mountains and fish in Little Redfish Lake. Later in the season, he could even ski. Harriman had invited Hemingway to stay at his resort free-of-charge along with some of the other celebrities of the day—among them Dorothy Parker and actors Gary Cooper and Ingrid Bergman—because his enormous fame would bring the resort some much needed publicity. The venture

Hemingway displays a brace of rainbow trout while on vacation in Sun Valley, Idaho, 1939. The following year, his second marriage ended in divorce, and he married the journalist Martha Gellhorn.

worked; stargazers arrived from every state in the country to see the famous patrons of Harriman's lodge.

Hemingway could not truly enjoy his surroundings during the summer of 1939, however. He was working furiously at his new novel, a novel he was under tremendous pressure to finish. Knowing now that the Spanish Civil War was only a prelude to a greater global conflict, he was racing to finish the book before the next round of warfare started and made his novel irrelevant even before it was published. But more important, he wanted to reclaim his title as the greatest writer of the age, a title he had lost after the series of critical failures following *A Farewell to Arms*:

> *I've worked at [the new novel] solid for seventeen months. This one had to be all right or I had to get out of the line, because my last job,* To Have and Have Not, *was not so good. For seventeen months I wrote no short stories or articles—nothing to earn a penny. I'm broke.*[11]

The incessant labor was beginning to wear Hemingway down in the early months of 1940. In a letter to Charles Scribner sent in February, it is evident that the pressure of writing—combined with the defeat of the Loyalists and the deterioration of his marriage—had succeeded in making Hemingway as full of dread and hopelessness as he had been in the early years of the 1930s, just before he had written "The Snows of Kilimanjaro":

> *Charlie there is no future in anything. I hope you agree. That is why I like it at a war. Every day and every night there is a strong possibility that you will get killed and not have to write. I have to write to be happy, whether I get paid for it or not. But it is a hell of a disease to be born with.*[12]

But after all the work, suffering under the enormous pressure of having to write a classic, Hemingway had finally produced another masterpiece. *For Whom the Bell Tolls* was published in October of 1940 and was immediately hailed by the reviewers as the best thing he had ever done. In November, it was named as the main selection of the Book-of-the-Month Club. It sold 135,000 copies in its first printing through November; 189,000 copies in its second printing through December; 491,000 copies in its third printing through April, and continued to sell for years—the biggest seller since *Gone With the Wind.* In January, Paramount Pictures bought the rights to make *For Whom the Bell Tolls* into a movie starring Hemingway's friends Gary Cooper and Ingrid Bergman— Hemingway held out for $100,000 in the deal. He was now a very wealthy man, and would never need Pauline's Uncle Gus again.

Critics raved about the novel's precision and honesty. It is the story of Robert Jordan, an American explosives expert sent into the mountains of Spain to destroy a bridge before Franco's army can escape a Loyalist attack. Within the framework of this ordinary war tale, Hemingway managed to expose the brutality and treachery that plagued both sides in the war. His writing was as clear and as sharp as ever, and the suspense of the story was carefully built up through each successive chapter of the longest book he would ever write. He was very careful to construct distinct and individual characters among the band of guerrillas Jordan enlists to help him with his task—a band that included the ruthless leader Pablo, the humble old man Anselmo, and Pilar—the strongest female character Hemingway ever created—who is responsible for holding the band together. If the book has a weakness, it is in the inevitable love story Hemingway wove through the narrative. Jordan's love interest, the beautiful peasant girl Maria, is passive to a fault, as weak as Pilar is strong, much like the other female characters in Hemingway's work. But after the critics called this flaw to the public's attention, they had nothing left but the highest praise.

But even though Hemingway was at the top of his writing form in 1939, he was having new psychological problems due to his alcoholism—a troublesome nervousness and paranoia—and his marriage was slipping from his grasp. He lived with Gellhorn almost all the time since his return from the war. But by Christmas of 1939, he was beginning to feel lonely and regretted his horrible treatment of his loving wife. He therefore left Gellhorn in Sun Valley and returned home to Key West to spend the holidays with his real family. But when he arrived, he found the house vacant. Pauline had already moved into a Manhattan apartment to escape the shambles of her marriage. Hemingway stayed in the empty house over Christmas night but packed some of his things the next morning and moved permanently into Finca Vigìa. The conchs, who had very traditional ideas about the roles of men and women in marriage, had already sided with Pauline in the domestic battle and promised to make Hemingway uncomfortable if he stayed. In early November of 1940; he divorced Pauline, and on November 21 he married Martha in Cheyenne, Wyoming. A justice of the peace presided over the ceremony. Pauline won custody of the children in the divorce, but they continued to see their father frequently for hunting trips and late nights of alcohol consumption.

For their honeymoon, Martha convinced Ernest to accept a reporting assignment with the New York liberal paper *PM* and accompany her to China, where they could cover the Sino-Japanese War together. (Martha was again writing for *Collier's*.) In the months and years leading up to this war, Japan had been adopting increasingly aggressive policies toward its neighbors in the Pacific Ocean. In 1940, in another dress rehearsal before the big show of World War II, Japan invaded China. Simultaneously, a civil war erupted among the Chinese as Mao and his fellow Communist revolutionaries clashed with the Nationalist government of Chiang Kai-shek. Hemingway disliked this reporting assignment, which was dull and empty of passion after the excitement of the Spanish Civil War. But he was able to travel through Hong Kong, Canton, Chunking, and Rangoon during his brief stay and developed some close ties with Communist advisors, American and British observers, Japanese and Chinese officers, and a multitude of other factions involved in the complicated war. And he learned a great deal about Asian culture.

The stiff competition for stories between Ernest and Martha had an adverse effect on their relationship and would continue to haunt them for the remainder of their marriage. Even though Hemingway disliked his work, he was careful to blaze his own trail as a journalist. His greatest success came when he was the first foreign reporter to do extensive research on the capabilities of the Chinese army. No doubt Martha was jealous of the accomplishment, just as Ernest was jealous of his wife's major stories. But in a special reporting coup, both Hemingways were granted an exclusive interview with the Chinese leader Chiang Kai-shek, perhaps easing the mounting tensions between them. The tensions mounting in the rest of the world, however, were not so easy to soothe.

AN ISOLATED HERO

CHAPTER VIII

"Tell me about it," Johnson said. "Were the Berlitz undergraduates a wild lot? What about all this necking and petting? Were there many smoothies? Did you ever run into Scott Fitzgerald?"

—Homage to Switzerland

ESIDES THE ENORMOUS success of *For Whom the Bell Tolls* in the early part of the decade, Ernest Hemingway received very little good news in the 1940s. One by one the symbols of his youth were dropping away, leaving the energetic writer with a feeling of loneliness more severe than he had ever known. Too old now for the fast-paced lifestyle he had made famous, but too stubborn to admit that those days were over, Hemingway found himself at the turning point of his life and his career. But faced with the choice between a dignified old age and the action he had always craved, Hemingway was still choosing the action. He was most alive on the battlefields, or on the hunt, or chasing a giant marlin through the Gulf of Mexico in *Pilar*. Like the bullfighters in *Death in the Afternoon*, he was most alive when the action was life-threatening. The safer, easier events of modern life only left him with time to think about his weakening powers as a writer and turned his attention to alcohol.

Hemingway received a new lesson in mortality in the early

Hemingway reunites with his old friend, the bookseller Sylvia Beach, in Paris in 1944.

1940s, as the great figures of his past were growing old and dying. William Butler Yeats and Ford Madox Ford, the stalwarts of a pre–World War I writing style, died in 1939. Hemingway's first supporter, Sherwood Anderson, and one of his harshest critics, Virginia Woolf, both died in 1941. Hemingway's friend James Joyce also died in 1941. But the real blow came during the Christmas holidays in 1940, when Hemingway received the news of Scott Fitzgerald's death. Fitzgerald died of a heart attack on December 21, 1940. He was only forty-four years old, but his severe drinking problem and the emotional devastation he suffered after Zelda's mental collapse had weakened his body as well as his mind. Hemingway's first reaction to the news was characteristically stoic and accepting. Then he became judgmental, sending letters to Max Perkins describing Fitzgerald's faults as a writer and a person in the hope that Perkins was now better able to analyze future writers of Fitzgerald's talent and temperament:

> *Scott died inside himself at around the age of thirty or thirty-five and his creative powers died somewhat later. This last book [Fitzgerald's last* was The Great Tycoon*] was written long after his creative power was dead and he was just beginning to find out what things were about.*[1]

But years later, when he was no longer jealous of Fitzgerald's talent or scornful of his behavior, Hemingway would take an active interest in Fitzgerald's legacy. He and Perkins would even plan to release a volume of Fitzgerald's letters, to present the public with the real man they knew and respected. Despite his unfair treatment of Fitzgerald in his writings, Hemingway would remember their friendship fondly in later years, when Fitzgerald's death became a symbol for his own lost youth.

As Hemingway mourned the loss of his friends and the world's greatest literary figures, the rest of the world was preparing to suffer the greater losses of the Second World War. On September 1, 1939, Hitler ignored the year-old agreement he had signed with Minister Neville Chamberlain at Munich and invaded Poland. The island-nation of Japan was threatening the rest of Asia in its search for land and natural resources. When Ernest and Martha were moving through Hawaii on their way home from China, they noticed that American war planes and battleships at the military base in Pearl Harbor were dangerously grouped together and susceptible to attack. Soon after they expressed their concern to military authorities in Hawaii, Pearl Harbor was indeed attacked and destroyed by Japanese fighter planes—on December 7, 1941. The United States had not been invaded by a foreign military force since the War of 1812, and President Roosevelt needed no other reason to send American troops into combat against both Japan and its European allies Germany and Italy.

When Congress declared war on the Axis powers in late

1941, Hemingway was living a relatively quiet life in Cuba, taking some time off after the nonstop excitement of the years following the Spanish Civil War. But now, with a new war erupting and the very real threat of fascism spreading to the far reaches of the globe, Martha was certain that Ernest would shake off his laziness and get involved. She encouraged him to travel with her to Europe, to use his boundless skills as a writer and contribute to the war effort as a reporter. He had already seen the value of his celebrity during the Spanish Civil War and now, Martha argued, he would be working for his own country. But Hemingway was less interested in writing at this point in his life, and more concerned with hands-on participation. Approaching middle age, he was still not content to sit at a desk and write stories for the noncombatants reading about the war back in the States. So he rejected Martha's suggestion and formulated his own plan, once again entering a war on his own terms.

In the early months of 1942, he approached his friend Spruille Braden, the American ambassador to Cuba, with a plan of action. At the time, the Caribbean Sea was swarming with people who supported the Fascists in Europe and would have supported a Fascist invasion of North America—a serious threat to America's safety after the Pearl Harbor disaster. Hemingway recognized the danger these local Fascists presented, so he proposed that he work as a spy among them, finding the Nazi supporters and reporting them to the American government. No American knew the Caribbean people or their cultures as well as "Mr. Ernest" and no one was as well equipped to learn their secrets. Braden approved the idea. With embassy support, Hemingway recruited six full-time agents and twenty spies from the Cuban underworld—jai alai players, gamblers, and vagrants—who worked among the people of Cuba and the neighboring islands. Hemingway gave his band the code name "Crook Factory," and they operated from May of 1942 to April of 1943, although their effect on the spread of nazism in the Western Hemisphere was negligible. Nevertheless, Hemingway's "Crook Factory" was without precedent in American history. No other American celebrity had ever had enough political influence to involve himself so deeply in international politics. Of course, certain agencies of the federal government objected to the use of a novelist in matters of national security. J. Edgar Hoover, head of the Federal Bureau of Investigation—who had already been watching Hemingway's movements since his past support for Stalin and the Communists during the Spanish Civil War—now expressed his concern about Hemingway in memos passed throughout Washington:

> *I of course realize the complete undesirability of this sort of a connection or relationship. Certainly Hemingway is the last man, in my estimation, to be used in any such capacity [as a spy ring]. His judgment is not of the best, and if his sobriety is the same as it was some years ago, that is certainly questionable.*[2]

In time, after the "Crook Factory" failed to produce results, most government officials including Hoover ceased to take Hemingway seriously. And Martha became downright scornful of the "Crook Factory," which she thought of as Hemingway's childish attempt to be young again. Only Ambassador Braden seemed to have any lasting faith in Hemingway's project. Fortunately, Ambassador Braden was the only one who mattered to Hemingway at the time.

After the Crook Factory's failure, Hemingway thought of a new way to enter the escalating conflict without leaving for the battlefields of Europe. German submarines had entered the Caribbean Sea in 1942 and were harassing American ships engaged in the vital trade with Central and South America. Hemingway now proposed to outfit *Pilar* with military weapons and search for the German submarines himself.

Once again, the ambassador was as enthralled as Hemingway with the idea of a roving submarine destroyer disguised as a fishing boat—although it was absurd to think that a fishing boat could defeat a submarine in combat. Braden immediately convinced John W. Thomason, chief of naval intelligence in Central America, to donate machine guns, grenades, and bombs to Hemingway's venture and even commissioned a marine to report to Hemingway for duty.

Martha was now even more furious with her husband for his recklessness, but Ernest ignored her objections. He assembled a crew of Cubans, some of his drinking buddies, and his two younger sons, and set out to do battle. Unfortunately, or perhaps fortunately, Hemingway did not encounter a single submarine at a range close enough for a confrontation, although some of his reports to the U.S. military about German positions proved helpful. Then on the last day of the submarine hunt, Hemingway spotted a black bulge on the horizon. Through his binoculars, he could see a massive submarine hull rising from the water. He prepared his crew for an engagement with the enemy. Gregory Hemingway, only twelve years old at the time, moved to his position in the bow of *Pilar* and cocked his hunting rifle, ready for a real military engagement. (He was using the same rifle his mother, Pauline, had used during the now-legendary African safari.) But the submarine was retreating from them, instead of approaching as originally supposed, and it was soon out of sight. A dejected Hemingway turned to his youngest son and told him that someone else would have to retaliate against the Axis powers for the attack at Pearl Harbor:

> *Someone else will fight for me on the beaches. December seven, a day that will live in infamy, will be avenged by younger men. Hell, fix me a gin and tonic, will you Gig? We're heading home.*[3]

If anybody knew that Hemingway was too old for the fight

he sought, it was Martha. Somehow she knew that her husband, the world-famous writer, was spending more time playing cards, drinking, and throwing grenades at an empty sea than he was spending in battle with the enemy. Not long after he returned from the submarine hunt, Martha reached her boiling point. She was fed up with Hemingway's thrill seeking and his self-promotion, she was fed up with his childish recklessness, and she was fed up with the fifty cats that roamed Finca Vigìa and received more of Hemingway's attention than she did.

Seeking to escape her husband, Martha accepted a proposal from *Collier's* to begin a new reporting tour, covering the combat of World War II from Europe to Africa. But Hemingway was not to be outdone by anyone, least of all his wife. Following Martha's sudden departure from Finca Vigìa, Hemingway put in his own call to *Collier's* and offered the magazine his services as a reporter. Hemingway knew that the editors would have to make a choice between Martha, a respected journalist, and himself, the world-famous novelist of modern warfare. And it was certain that they would choose him. His reputation alone would sell more magazines than Martha could sell with a Pulitzer Prize–winning article. Not long after Martha had arrived in Europe, she found herself out of a job. Hemingway successfully destroyed his third marriage. But this time, he was sure he was blameless:

> *I think no one gets a very accurate or credible account from either party to a broken marriage. Certainly I am not giving one...Anyone confusing a handsome and ambitious girl with the Queen of Heaven should be punished as a fool.*[4]

Hemingway arrived in London in May of 1944 to find the city devastated after numerous bombings by the German airforce. But in the midst of the destruction, he was surrounded by friends and was pleased with his decision to join the news-

A devastated aread around Stratford Street, London, in the aftermath of a German air attack in 1944.

men covering the combat. He was even reunited with many of his old cronies. Lewis Galantière, his first friend from the Paris days, was in town, as was the Spanish Civil War photographer Robert Capa, the writer William Saroyan, Hemingway's younger brother Leicester—who served alternately as a member of the military and Hemingway's private secretary—and the novelist Irwin Shaw. Shaw made the greatest impression on Hemingway in the early days of his London assignment, not because the two writers had anything in common, but because Shaw was the companion of a woman named Mary Welsh Monks who immediately caught Hemingway's fancy.

Mary Welsh was born in 1908 in Bemidji, Minnesota, and studied journalism at Northwestern University outside of Chicago. A petite, oddly attractive blond with a sharp mind,

*Hemingway was
introduced to the American
journalist Mary Welsh in
London in 1944.*

she had worked for *The American Florist* and other small journals in the States before landing a job at the *London Daily
Express,* which eventually led to a prestigious position at the
London office of *Time* magazine. She was married to an
Australian journalist named Noel Monks when she met Shaw
and Hemingway in 1944, but the two were constantly separated because of their reporting jobs and the marriage was
breaking up. Shaw and Welsh were very close in the early
spring of 1944, but Hemingway moved in and pushed Shaw
aside, winning Welsh over with the most outrageous proposal
he could think of. "I don't know you," he said to her only days
after their first meeting, "but I want to marry you."[5]

   In late May, still in London, Hemingway and some
friends were driving home from a party during a blackout
when the driver could no longer see the streets and drove
the car into a steel water tank. Hemingway was the only

passenger injured in the crash, but he had a major concussion and a gash on his head that required fifty-seven stitches. (It would be the first of three concussions in the next two years.) Martha made one last attempt to be a caring wife after the accident and rushed to Hemingway's bedside in the hospital. She expected to find him in need of her care and sympathy. Instead, she found him surrounded by his rowdy friends, passing around a bottle of champagne. She immediately left the room, thinking that Hemingway had finally hit rock bottom and was the most immature forty-five-year-old man in the world. But Hemingway was not alone long. Mary Welsh immediately took Martha's place at his bedside.

It was Hemingway's good fortune to be released from the hospital on June 6, just as the Allied forces were beginning their final thrust to regain Europe from Hitler and the Nazis. After his foolish drinking bouts in the hospital, Hemingway redeemed himself by racing to the battle front with the British Royal Air Force and working his way into the heart of the action in the French region of Normandy. As one fellow reporter remembered:

> *I'd lose him somewhere and I'd figure, 'I'm going to find Papa where the excitement is.' And I'd walk down the street and hear his voice, 'Bring me a bottle of your finest wine, quickly!'. . .I thought he was one of the happiest men I ever knew, a guy with a great zest for life and who enjoyed every minute of it.*[6]

In truth, Hemingway was not as happy as he looked. Many problems would soon crop up in his life, problems that began long before he entered the theater of World War II. But for the moment, he was content to be back with the troops. He was back on his proving-ground and up to his old antics. In one report to *Collier's*, he claimed to have helped the U.S. generals plan the landing and the D-Day invasion of the French coast at Omaha Beach. Later, he would make the more outrageous claim that he had been one of the thousands of Americans landed on the beach. Even for Hemingway such a landing would have been difficult to arrange given the wartime restrictions on the movements of journalists on the battlefields. But Martha actually did manage to be among the troops landed at Omaha. She hid herself on a transport vessel heading into battle, and the American military was not aware of her presence on the ship until it was too late to turn her away. Hemingway would always be jealous of Martha's reporting coup during the D-Day invasion.

During the invasion of Normandy, Hemingway received his second concussion in a matter of weeks when he and Robert Capa accidentally drove a car into a roadside ditch. This time, Hemingway made a speedy recovery and, contrary to the rules of the Geneva Convention, which prohibited

A bearded Hemingway jokes with U.S. troops around the time of the Allied invasion of Normandy.

journalists from taking part in actual combat, he tried to help Allied troops on the march toward Paris. Serving as an advance man for the Fourth Infantry Division of the U.S. Army, under the command of Major General Raymond O. Barton, Hemingway scouted the area directly before the troops to make sure their path was clear of Nazi interference. In this project, he worked alongside his new friend Colonel Charles "Buck" Lanham of the Twenty-second Regiment. After scouting the land, Hemingway was given a small troop of men and set up a military government in the town of Rambouillet, twenty miles outside of Paris. Hemingway was the governor of the town for days until the Allies successfully regained Paris. He marched into the city with the victorious liberators and joined the raucous celebration of the city's liberation. Predictably, Hemingway went straight to the Ritz Hotel, and claimed to "liberate" its luxurious bar by ordering drinks for himself and all of his companions. For his part in the reoccupation of Paris, in violation of the Geneva Convention agreements, Hemingway was later called to a military hearing to decide if he should be punished. Buck Lanham spoke up in Hemingway's defense, however, and the writer was released without punishment, even though the entire city of Paris knew that Hemingway had carried firearms and maps and had directed troops. As he had proven with his "Crook Factory" work, he had a knack for getting out of tight spots with the U.S. government.

Only weeks since the terrible car accident and his childish behavior at the hospital, Hemingway was once again a victorious hero. He stayed at the Ritz with Mary Welsh through the summer of 1944, spending time with his old friends Sylvia Beach and Picasso, and his new friends Jean-Paul Sartre and Simone de Beauvoir. He even had a brief meeting with Gertrude Stein. (Stein would die in Paris in 1946, at the age of 72.) But the great liberation party ended in the fall of 1944, when Hemingway followed Buck Lanham and the

Colonel Charles "Buck" Lanham leads his 22nd Regiment in an Allied offensive as a somewhat beleaguered Hemingway does his part for the war effort.

22nd Regiment to the Rhine River in Germany's Hürtgen Forest for the Allies final group of offensives against the Axis powers in Europe. The Hürtgen offensive was an awful experience for the American troops. The 22nd Regiment alone lost 300 men in the bloody forest campaign. Hemingway was understandably disturbed by the ordeal. In his letters to Welsh, he hinted at his new fear of warfare, but of course he chose to describe only his few heroic moments in detail:

> *stone cold and with nothing to drink...I get the old feeling of immortality back I used to have when I was 19—right in the middle of a really bad shelling...it doesn't make any sense—But it's a lovely feeling.*[7]

On December 16, the remnants of Lanham's 22nd Regiment

left the dense German forest for Luxembourg and came up against the last German counter-offensive of the war, the Battle of the Bulge. Hemingway might have experienced this battle if he had not met Martha at the front. She even seemed to be waiting for him there, waiting to ask him for a divorce. After a few, angry meetings not far from the lines of battle, the details of the divorce were finalized—according to Cuban law, Hemingway kept Finca Vigìa, all of the cats, and most of their mutual possessions. The only other good news that Hemingway received about his personal life as the Allied victory drew nearer concerned his oldest son. Bumby was now in his twenties and had enlisted with the U. S. military. At the beginning of the D-Day invasion, he had been ordered to parachute behind enemy lines and engage the Germans from the rear. He never completed his mission. He was wounded and captured by the Nazis almost as soon as he touched ground and thereafter held as a prisoner of war. But now, in the winter of 1944, Bumby was released and returned safely to his family. Hemingway was, of course, very proud of his soldier son and relieved by his return.

At the end of the European war, Hemingway returned to his home in Cuba. Mary Welsh was finishing up a number of her own *Time* articles and did not arrive until March of 1946, delaying their marriage until the fourteenth of that month. It was a new marraige for a changed world. The Fascists, Hemingway's bitter enemies, were effectively wiped out in 1945. Hitler committed suicide as the Allies rolled through his once-powerful empire, and Mussolini was executed in a public hanging orchestrated by the very people who had supported his rapid rise to power. But these victories were bitter-sweet for the United States and its Allies. If the trench warfare of World War I had changed the way people thought about their world—a change that Hemingway was so swift to document in his fiction—then the destruction of World War II had pushed people's fears to their extremes. The mass executions at the Nazi concentration camps and the annihilation of entire cities at the close of the war—including the Allied firebombing of the German city of Dresden and the United States' use of atomic bombs on the Japanese cities of Hiroshima and Nagasaki—suggested a new kind of warfare, and the declining value of human life. Of course, the literary community responded to the changes with new writing techniques and new ideas for stories. But Hemingway, the famous voice of the Lost Generation, steered himself clear of the new conflicts that the war introduced into literature. He was content to continue his old life of drinking and fishing in Cuba, content to write on the old themes even though he could feel the world passing him by. Slowly, he was losing touch with the new realities of American life.

Meanwhile, his friend and mentor Ezra Pound was also losing touch with the modern world. Pound, however, was suffering from psychological problems as well as from a literary detachment. He had become erratic and irrational in his later years. Some of his closest friends were even afraid the great poet had become insane. Their fears seemed justified when he continued to support Mussolini's regime in Italy in spite of the Fascists' heinous war crimes. Compounding his own problems in the public eye, he had broadcasted his own views of the war on a Fascist radio station in April of 1943. (Pound was still living in Italy during the war.) Among the outrageous requests he made during the broadcasts were those for the legal execution of the world's Jewish population and for the trial and execution of President Franklin Roosevelt. After the Allied victory in Europe, Pound was arrested for treason by the U.S. military and held in a cage in the Italian city of Pisa until he could be brought to trial in the States. But he was declared mentally unfit for trial by military psychologists and was moved to St. Elizabeth's Hospital in Washington, D.C., where he underwent treatment for twelve years. Hemingway, T. S. Eliot, Archibald MacLeish, and the remaining writers of Lost Generation Paris condemned Pound's broadcasts as the rantings of a madman. Still, they supported their friend publicly as a truly kind man suffering from a serious mental disease. Pound was finally released from St. Elizabeth's in 1958 and died in 1972 at the age of 87. He outlived Hemingway by eleven years.

While Pound was imprisoned for his disturbing views regarding America's role in the war, Hemingway was once again honored by the U.S. government as a war hero. On June 16, 1947 at the American Embassy in Havana, a U.S. military attaché awarded Hemingway with the Bronze Star for his service to the nation as a foreign correspondent—a far cry from his earlier trial for violation of the Geneva Convention agreements. But Hemingway could hardly enjoy the new recognition in the summer of 1947. He would soon hear the news that John and Katy Dos Passos had been in a car accident on Cape Cod. Katy was killed and John lost an eye. Although Hemingway and Dos Passos had not spoken in years, the accident was yet another example of the tragedy invading his once happy life. And Hemingway received more horrible news from New York later in that summer. Max Perkins had died of a heart attack. By 1947, Perkins was one of the most important editors in the world. But he was terribly overworked, which contributed to his rapidly declining health. At the time of his death, Hemingway had been sending him installments of a new novel he was working on, a novel about relationships between men and women entitled *The Garden of Eden*. Loosely based on his recent experiences with Martha and Mary, it promised to be a different kind of book than the one Hemingway's fans were used to. But a grieving Hemingway put the book aside after Perkins's death, and never picked it up again. (It was finally published, in its unfinished form, in 1986.)

Now in his fourth marriage, without many of the friends and associates that had peopled the last twenty years of his life, and nearly ten years since he had published anything of lasting value, Hemingway faced his darkest depression yet. To make matters worse, his constant drinking was beginning to affect both his behavior and his health. He was noticing signs of heart trouble and high blood pressure, aggravated by his new tendency to gain weight. Occasionally, he would hear a ringing in his ears. Edema was setting in and his joints began to stiffen. And his already bad temper was getting worse. Though Mary was the attentive wife that Martha had never been, she and Ernest argued frequently, and he had even begun to threaten her physically.

Against this backdrop of mental and physical decline, Ernset and Mary took a winter vacation to Venice in 1948. He loved the ancient city that he had helped to defend back in 1919, with its crowded canals and its exquisite architecture. One day, during a duck hunt in the marshes outside of the city, Hemingway's luck seemed to change again. Something

Hemingway visits Venice, Italy, with his fourth wife, Mary (left), and his muse, Adriana Ivancich, in 1950.

almost mystical happened. Forty-nine-year-old Ernest Hemingway was confronted by a new symbol of youth—he was introduced to the beautiful nineteen-year-old daughter of an important Venetian family, Adriana Ivancich. He immediately fell in love. Ivancich shared many of Hemingway's interests in poetry and the visual arts, and they carried on a six-year correspondence after Hemingway left Venice. But she never returned his affections. Nevertheless, Hemingway was quick to acknowledge that Ivancich had a profound effect on the final years of his writing career. In one letter to Ivancich, he even described her as an inspiration for his later work:

> *You have given me back the possibility of writing again, and I shall be grateful to you for it always. I have been able to finish my book and I have given your face to the protagonist. Now I will write another book for you, and it will be my most beautiful book. It will be about an old man and the sea.*[8]

The first book Hemingway refers to in this passage became *Across the River and Into the Trees*, which he began writing as soon as he returned to Cuba from Venice. (Ivancich's brother served as her substitute on the voyage home, accompanying the Hemingways back to Cuba and staying at Finca Vigìa in the following years.) The second book, *The Old Man and the Sea*, became Hemingway's last classic and was published in 1952.

Across the River and Into the Trees is the story of Richard Cantwell, a professional soldier and a veteran of World War I, the Spanish Civil War, and World War II. In the novel, Cantwell returns to the city he loves most on earth, Venice, first for a duck hunt and then to see his nineteen-year-old love Renata, a Venetian countess. Cantwell is nearing the end of his life, and he uses his vacation and his love affair with Renata as an opportunity to reflect on his past. The action of Hemingway's previous novels is therefore replaced by meditations on war and love, and on the fabled city of Venice. As a result, *Across the River* is Hemingway's slowest novel, and most critics considered it his worst. Published in 1950, so soon after the victories of World War II, some patriotic critics objected to the book's harsh criticisms of America's generals. Others accused the book of having a flawed structure and little plot development. Still others accused Cantwell, and Hemingway, of adopting a false posture of aged wisdom. Even Ivancich criticized the book, claiming that Renata was more like Hemingway's fantasy woman than a real character. Hemingway's only defense of the book was that it was misunderstood. The real story of *Across the River* was to be found beneath the surface of the narrative, he said. The meaning of the book was implied rather than stated:

> *Sure, they can say anything about nothing happening in* Across the River, *but all that happens is the defense of the lower Piave, the breakthrough in Normandy, the taking of Paris and the destruction of the 22nd Infantry Regiment in Hurtgen forest, plus a man loves a girl and dies.*[9]

For most readers, however, a clearer notion of how these events played upon the narrative would have greatly improved the novel. As it appeared, most critics and readers were greatly disappointed by the long-awaited follow-up to *For Whom the Bell Tolls* and were ready to condemn Hemingway as a writer who had used up his talent. At this point, even Hemingway was beginning to believe that his career as a writer was finished. His depression worsened, as did his alcohol dependency. He no longer seemed able to stop his own decline.

THE FINAL BATTLE

CHAPTER IX

Now, without thinking any further, he would go home to his room. He would lie in bed and finally, with daylight, he would go to sleep. After all, he said to himself, it is probably only insomnia. Many must have it.
—*A Clean Well-Lighted Place*

LTHOUGH HEMINGWAY HAD taken a ten-year hiatus from novel writing after completing *For Whom the Bell Tolls,* he was far from unproductive during that decade. He was a prolific war correspondent for *Collier's* during World War II and continued to publish short stories in *Esquire* and other important journals throughout the 1940s. But there was a noticeable decline in the quality of these later stories, especially when compared with masterpieces like "The Snows of Kilimanjaro." By the early 1950s, his writer's block assumed serious proportions and he dreaded the loss of his talent. Of course, this was not the first time he worried about his writing ability. He had kicked and scratched his way back to literary preeminence many times in his career, always coming up with a masterpiece when he needed it most. This time, however, even he did not know if his skills would return. At fifty years of age, he was less resilient and more irritable than ever before. And as a reluctant public figure, he was forced to deal with the distrac-

The September 1, 1952 cover of Life *magazine, in which Hemingway's short story "The Old Man and the Sea" was published.*

tions of his celebrity life—distractions that multiplied with each year of his rising fame. For a man whose only true love was his writing, these distractions were more than mere annoyances. In fact, they were maddening.

As Hemingway aged and his production as a writer slackened, literary scholars sensed that the time was ripe for a coherent study of his work. Like the vultures drawn to Harry Walden's deathbed in "The Snows of Kilimanjaro," aspiring writers, professors, and biographers joined the multitudes of gossips, stargazers, and autograph seekers who followed Hemingway's every movement. Finca Vigìa was flooded with young academics hoping to write the true story of

Hemingway's life. As expected, Hemingway discouraged most interviews and dismissed most of the writers as mercenaries hoping to cash in on his fame. However, a few of the biographers were allowed into the Hemingway inner circle—if only for a short time. Carlos Baker, a professor at Princeton, joined the ranks as the only biographer authorized by the Hemingway family. Charles Fenton, whose explorations into Hemingway's early life at Oak Park caused an endless dispute between himself and his subject, was also on hand in the early 1950s. But it was A. E. Hotchner who had the longest relationship with America's favorite writer, perhaps because he did not write his Hemingway book until after Hemingway died. In addition to these three tag-a-longs, Hemingway was also learning to handle the American and European journalists who were constantly looking for a good quotation from him on almost any topic, from politics to alcohol. And of course, there were the usual celebrity visits to Finca Vigìa. Even the British nobles, the Duke and Duchess of Windsor, called upon the Hemingways during this eventful period. Hemingway's life was never devoid of excitement, but it was increasingly devoted to things other than writing in the 1950s. Hemingway tried desperately to halt this trend.

Before he met Adriana Ivancich and began work on *Across the River and Into the Trees* in 1948, Hemingway had started an ambitious set of three related stories devoted to the land, the air, and the sea. He called the trilogy *Islands in the Stream*. The stories are centered on a character named Thomas Hudson, whose exciting life bears a striking resemblance to Hemingway's own life, including Hudson's own brief stint as a submarine hunter in the Caribbean. No longer able to rely on his dulled imagination, Hemingway was disappointed with his first attempts to tell Hudson's story and shelved the manuscript. He resumed work on *Islands* after the publication of *Across the River and Into the Trees*, and he tried his best to put aside all of life's distractions at writing time, between the hours of

7:00 A.M. and noon. For the most part, work on the trilogy was a constant struggle, and the words would not flow smoothly. By 1951, Hemingway was happy only with the trilogy's epilogue—a story he had heard years before about an old man and a giant marlin. It was the second story he had promised to write for Ivancich in the letter he had written in 1948.

Mary was Hemingway's typist while he was working on *Islands in the Stream*. She was not impressed with most of the writing that passed her desk. But then she came to the epilogue, the new story about the man and the fish. She read it in one sitting, and it gave her goosebumps. It was the story that fulfilled his promise as a writer, she told him. Hemingway then sent the draft of the story to Carlos Baker. Baker's reaction was as enthusiastic as Mary's. The new story, titled *The Old Man and the Sea*, was astounding. Hemingway now sensed that he had created another masterpiece and decided to publish the story as a novella, entirely separate from the labored *Islands in the Stream*. It may have been the wisest decision of his entire career—*Islands* was not published until 1970, eleven years after Hemingway's death.

The Old Man and the Sea is Hemingway's most-beautiful work, a parable about human survival in a hostile world. It is based on a common theme in Hemingway's work, expressed most succinctly in the old man's thoughts as "a man can be destroyed but not defeated."[1] The old man in the tale, Santiago, was once the greatest fisherman in the Cuban port of Cojimar. Now at the end of his life, he knows only bad luck. Nevertheless, Santiago heads out to sea in a small boat, searching for the giant marlin that would restore his wounded pride. After weeks of failure, he finally hooks the greatest fish he has ever seen and, alone on the open sea, wins the ensuing battle. The fish is caught. But after Santiago lashes the marlin to the side of his boat, sharks are drawn to the carcass and tear apart the old man's prize. Santiago is forced to fight off the sharks and captain the boat simultaneously. When he returns to Cojimar, there his nothing left of his trophy but a giant skeleton, stripped clean by the sharks. Though it is certainly not an optimistic ending, Hemingway manages to keep the old man's dignity intact through his defeat. The old man is saved by the pureness of his heart.

Once again Hemingway managed to follow up a disastrous performance in *Across the River* with a classic. But *The Old Man and the Sea* would be Hemingway's last successful comeback. Perhaps Hemingway even had a sense of his imminent decline in 1952, in the months preceding the release of his new novella—which was printed in its entirety, in a single issue of *Life* magazine. More like an excited schoolboy than an experienced writer, Hemingway was terribly anxious to get the book to his readers. He even asked *Life* editor-in-chief Henry Luce for an advance copy of the magazine to settle his nerves: "Is there any chance I could have an advance copy of the magazine—to show no one—just to get the waiting over?"[2] On September 1, 1952, the wait ended. A small crowd gathered around a Times Square newsstand in New York City, waiting for the delivery of the *Life* issue with the new Hemingway novella, just as Americans a century earlier waited on the docks in New York Harbor for the newest Charles Dickens novel to arrive by ship.[3] More than 5 million copies of the magazine were sold over the next two days. Hemingway's face was on the front page.

Released a few days later in book form, *The Old Man and the Sea* became a September selection of the Book-of-the-Month Club and was a six-month best-seller. In fact, it was Hemingway's most-successful book ever. Even he was suprised. "Don't you think it is a strange damn story that it should affect all of us (me especially) the way it does?" he wrote to Henry Luce.[4] Hollywood producers fought for the rights to make a movie adaptation of the tale and Leland Hayward won the battle. Spencer Tracy was cast as Santiago,

Hemingway and the actor Spencer Tracy get acquainted on the set of the filming of The Old Man and the Sea.

and Hemingway was paid $150,000 for his work as a technical advisor during filming in the Caribbean and off the coast of Peru. (As an advisor, he made suggestions about how to authenticate the fishing scenes. He even tried to catch a giant marlin for the film. But, to Hemingway's disappointment, a rubber replica was used in the final version.)

In addition to all of the popular acclaim it received, *The Old Man and the Sea* was praised by the critics as the beginning of a new and more sensitive phase in Hemingway's writing. They emphasized its symbolic power as a moral tale, although Hemingway continued to publicly deny the presence of either symbols or morals in his literature. William Faulkner even accused him of finding God and religion in his new story.[5] The overwhelming majority of readers and critics praised the novella as a literary wonder, a poem written in prose. Hemingway could not have been happier with the success of his book. He needed to write a classic to maintain his stature as America's favorite writer, and he had written a classic. In fact, he had written a winner. While fishing on *Pilar* on May 4, 1953, Hemingway learned that his novella had earned him the Pulitzer Prize, his first major, nonmilitary award, but not the last award that *The Old Man and the Sea* would win for him.

Still, there was a downside to the success of *The Old Man and the Sea*. The scholars, mercenaries, and photographers now increased their efforts to move in on Hemingway's life. As Hemingway learned in 1952, everyone loves a winner. The pressures of fame became unbearable, and Hemingway grew restless. He planned an escape:

> *I want to get out of here as soon as possible. This was the first time I ran into the responsibilities of mass circulation. I have tried to handle them but I know I have not done it as well as I should.*[6]

But the now-suffocating intrusion of the public into his private life was only one of the problems he wished to escape in 1952. There were other more serious issues to plague his conscience and dampen the victory he had achieved with *The Old Man and the Sea*. On June 28, 1951, Grace Hemingway died. In the last years of her life, she had become slightly senile and Hemingway had made an attempt to repair their ruined relationship. There was little improvement, however, and Hemingway did not attend his mother's funeral, although he did arrange the ceremonies over the telephone from Cuba. Then, on October 1, 1951, Hemingway received the even more shocking news that Pauline had died suddenly of a rare disorder of the adrenal glands. Her condition made her highly susceptible to increased levels of stress, so Hemingway blamed his son Gregory for her death—Gregory had recently been arrested in California for drug possession. But Hemingway's bitter fight with Pauline over the telephone on the previous night probably contributed to her fatal condition and made matters worse. In any event, Hemingway now had reason to regret his behavior following both Grace's and Pauline's deaths. But the most disheartening news of the year came on February 11, 1952, when Hemingway learned that his publisher and friend, Charles Scribner, had died of a heart attack. Scribner was now added to the list of former companions who had either died or had had relationship-ending quarrels with Hemingway, a list that included Max Perkins, John Dos Passos, Gertrude Stein, Scott Fitzgerald, and Sherwood Anderson. Except for his wife Mary, A. E. Hotchner, and a few of the other young men who latched on to him at the end of his life, Hemingway was mostly alone in the world by 1952. He was now the only remaining member of the great, Parisian literary circles of the 1920s, of which he had been the center attraction.

Gone too were his soldiering days. In June of 1950, the United States was drawn into yet another foreign war, this time in the divided nation of Korea. Earlier in that year, the Soviet Union and Communist China supported North Korea's invasion of Democratic South Korea, in the hope of spreading their own influence throughout Southeast Asia. President Harry S. Truman feared the spread of Soviet influence more than any other threat to America's safety in the early years of the cold war. As a result, U.S. troops and the armies of the United Nations were sent into combat in support of South Korea. The war ended in a stalemate in 1953, without either side gaining much territory. But Hemingway never joined the American effort. He was simply too old, at 52 years of age, to enjoy the action as he used to. Until now he had participated in every war available to him. But his age had suddenly become a factor in his decisions. The onset of middle age, combined with the string of deaths that marked the end of the Lost Generation and the increasing demands of fame were too much to handle. In the spring of 1952, Hemingway planned his escape. His great wish was to return to Africa and to the safari—the favorite setting of his glorious youth.

On June 24, 1952, Ernest, Mary, and a large entourage of newer acquaintances set sail on the S.S. *Flandre* to Le Havre in northern France. The party then traveled south to Spain for the summer festivals in Pamplona and Madrid. Hemingway was generally disappointed with the diminished quality of the bullfights that year, but he was also introduced to the greatest matador he had ever seen, a true diamond in the rough, Antonio Ordóñez. (Antonio was the son of Cayetano Ordóñez, the model for Pedro Romero of *The Sun Also Rises*.) Leaving Spain after the festivals, the Hemingways went on to Mombassa, Kenya, for a safari financed by *Look* magazine. *Look* agreed to subsidize the entire trip as payment for a pair of Hemingway's legendary articles about the hunt. It was just the kind of break Hemingway needed, a chance to regain his youth in a country he loved.

The safari began innocently enough. Philip Percival, the leader of Hemingway's first safari, came out of retirement specifically to join Hemingway on the hunt. Hemingway was also welcomed back by the Masai tribes he had befriended in the 1930s, who made him an honorary deputy in the fight against the lion packs threatening the Masai cattle herds. Amid all of the welcoming celebrations, Hemingway even managed to shoot a few leopards in the early weeks. But his eyesight had been failing him in recent years, and he and Percival spent an inordinate amount of time drinking in the afternoons. On a safari, those two things—poor eyesight and heavy drinking—were a formula for disaster. When disaster finally did strike, however, it was not even Hemingway's fault.

As Mary's Christmas present that year, Ernest chartered a small plane for a sight-seeing tour of the Belgian Congo. The

On safari in Africa in the early 1950s, Hemingway engages a local man in a mock boxing match to the amusement of several Masai tribesmen.

African wilderness was famous for its awesome geographical formations, its active volcanoes, and the colorful names of its landmarks: Ngorongoro Crater, the Mountains of the Moon, Lake Albert, Lake Victoria. Hemingway wanted to see it all. He remembered the effect of his first flight in Africa, when he passed Mount Kilimanjaro for the first time, and he hoped that a similar scene would inspire him to write again. This time he was disappointed. The plane took off on January 21, 1953 with a young pilot named Roy Marsh at the controls. On the first day of the trip, Marsh had problems with the engine but managed to clear Lake Victoria. The second day passed without incident. But on the third day, as they were flying over Murchison Falls in Uganda, the plane disturbed a flock of ibis. Marsh banked the plane to stay clear of the

A serious and accomplished big-game hunter, Hemingway poses here with a leopard he took down while on safari in Africa in the 1950s.

birds, but as he did so the wings of the plane snagged on a string of telegraph wires stretched across the falls. Marsh was forced to crash land. Thankfully, no one was seriously injured. Hemingway dislocated his shoulder and Mary broke two ribs, but they were healthy enough to survive a night in the wilderness, avoiding crocodiles and elephants lumbering in the night. Without a working radio, they had to wait until morning for a passing boat, the *Murchison*, to pick them up.

Back in the United States, newspapers were already printing headlines about the Hemingways' crash, reporting that both the writer and his wife were dead. (Hemingway would amuse himself for weeks after his return to Cuba, reading his own obituaries.) But as these reports were spinning off the presses, The *Murchison* was carrying the Hemingways and their pilot to Butiaba. Hemingway then chartered another plane, a De Havilland Rapide, to carry them to Entebbe, Uganda, where a press conference was scheduled to clear up any lingering doubts that he and his wife were still alive. But then real disaster struck. The De Havilland never left Butiaba. It merely lurched off of the runway for a few seconds before crashing back down into the pavement and bursting into flames—the Hemingways' second plane crash in as many days. Mary, Roy Marsh, and the De Havilland pilot all escaped the wreck with minor injuries. But Hemingway was slow to act and was trapped in the flames. Using his head and his good arm, he threw himself into the jammed cabin door repeatedly until he beat his way out of the burning plane.

Hemingway received very little medical attention that night, and in the morning he followed through with his plans to see his son Patrick for a fishing trip. (Patrick had fulfilled his lifelong dream and was now a professional hunter like Philip Percival.) Simultaneously, he dictated two articles about the crashes to Mary for publication in *Look* magazine. And he was somehow involved in an effort to put out a brushfire, which singed off most of his hair and gave him some minor burns.

But Hemingway was not able to continue his masquerade for very long. In truth, he was a very sick man after the crashes. He had sustained a series of agonizing injuries, the effects of which lingered for the rest of his life. When he returned to Venice after the safari and finally received the medical attention he so desperately needed, he learned that he had two cracked spinal disks, a dislocated right arm and shoulder, his tenth and most serious concussion—which resulted in a stream of cranial fluid leaking behind his left ear—a ruptured kidney, and a ruptured liver. The injuries, especially the concussion, were debilitating psychologically as well as physically.

Persistent pain made Hemingway violently irritable and sped up the emotional collapse that would culminate before the end of the decade. Mary was the primary victim of his anger, and they fought incessantly after the safari, although Hemingway would always be repentant later for his poor behavior. "I love Miss Mary truly," he once told a friend. "She knows this and it helps her to forgive me when I am in the wrong."[7] Hemingway was "in the wrong" often in subsequent years, so often in fact that even his closest friends would begin to question his sanity.

Before the final disaster of his life, however, Hemingway was destined to be a champion one final time. On October 28, 1954, the Finca Vigìa phone rang and Hemingway received the news he had hoped for ever since he had written *A Farewell to Arms*. The Swedish Academy voted to make Hemingway the year's winner of the Noble Prize for Literature. In its announcement, the Academy made special mention of his remarkable achievement in *The Old Man and the Sea*. Along with the tax-free award of $35,000, the Nobel Prize guaranteed that Hemingway would have a special place in literary history as an acknowledged master of his craft. It was a definite high point in Hemingway's life, but he was not ready for the subsequent publicity. Still recovering from the plane crashes, Hemingway was drinking heavily to ward off the severe pain of his injuries. (He was also working on a new safari piece called "African Journal," which would be published posthumously in *Sports Illustrated* in 1971–72.) In addition, he had always disliked public speaking and rejected most speaking engagements without hesitation, even when he was healthy. Therefore, when the Academy requested his presence at the award ceremony, Hemingway regretfully announced that he could not attend. Instead, he wrote a brief but heartfelt acceptance speech to be read at the Stockholm ceremony by John Cabot, the American ambassador to Sweden. Most of Hemingway's speech was devoted to the recognition of writers who did not win the award and to the debt that modern writers owe to their literary forebears:

> *For a true writer, each book should be a new beginning where he tries again for something that is beyond attainment. . .It is because we have had such great writers in the past that a writer is driven far out past where he can go, out to where no one can help him.*[8]

Hemingway knew that he could receive no greater recognition than the Noble Prize. Still, it was a bit of an anticlimax now that so many of his friends were not around to share his joy. And what little joy he was capable of feeling was muted by his physical deterioration. His pain was so great in October of 1952 that even he was talking about it, breaking his own code of dignified silence. In an understated letter to his old friend Chink Dorman-Smith, just days before his Nobel Prize was announced, he wrote, "I get tired of pain sometimes even if that is an ignoble feeling."[9]

For the next two years, Hemingway's life moved at a snail's pace. He was still working on *Islands in the Stream*, but only because he could not let himself give it up. He also continued to travel, though not as extensively as he once had. He had grown a full, white beard in recent years to protect his sensitive skin from the sun. But his unique facial hair made it easy for fans to spot him on a crowded street. As a result, a bearded Papa could not go anywhere in public without drawing a throng of well-wishers and autograph seekers. Usually, he opted to stay inside. He did work with Spencer Tracy on the movie version of *The Old Man and the Sea*, however, and in the summer of 1955, he traveled to Key West for the first time since his divorce from Pauline. Ostensibly, he returned to his old Whitehead Street house to attend to the financial matters that popped up after Pauline's death. But the trip was a bad idea. Alone in the house where he had written some of his greatest fiction, he was haunted by memories of his glorious past. Frequently now, he turned to vodka and Scotch for comfort.

In 1957, employees of the Ritz Hotel in Paris found two abandoned suitcases in the hotel basement. In the suitcases, Mary later claimed, were the notes and manuscripts that Hemingway had worked on during his early years in Paris. If her story is true, it explains why Hemingway set aside *Islands in the Stream* in that year and began work on his Paris memoir, *A Moveable Feast*. In this new book, Hemingway documented his earliest impressions of the great city in the 1920s, where he lived with his young wife Hadley and a head full of dreams. Scott Fitzgerald, Ezra Pound, Ford Madox Ford, and Gertrude Stein burst from the pages in Hemingway's accounts of conversations with the writers of the Lost Generation and the Jazz Age. In 1957, as his marriage to Mary deteriorated into a series of battles and his friends from the Lost Generation were either dead or far away, this Paris memoir took on the added importance of a psychological release for Hemingway. He fought off the ghosts of his past with each word he wrote. Some passages are therefore brutally honest while others have the ring of good fiction. But as in all of Hemingway's best work, the fiction and the truth combine to form an entertaining and lively account of the vital expatriate days.

Hemingway knew that this memoir would be read more closely by literary historians than any of his novels. And he was equally aware that his characterizations of Stein and Ford and Fitzgerald were absolutely libelous in places. To cover his tracks, he returned to the technique he adopted in the scandalous *To Have and Have Not* and wrote a disclaimer for the book's preface:

> *If the reader prefers, this book may be regarded as fiction. But there is always the chance that such a book of fiction may throw some light on what has been written as fact.*[10]

It is therefore possible to approach *A Moveable Feast* as a factual account of Parisian life, or as a fictional parody, or as the bitter writings of a spiteful man nearing the end of his life. Most accurately, it is all of the above.

"My nerves are shot to hell with pain, and that is not a thing I would tell anybody," Hemingway said to A. E. Hotchner in the late 1950s. "You look awful and the lousy pain shows on your face. So [press photographers] take photographs of you."[11] He never fully recovered from the injuries he suffered after the second plane crash in 1953. For a time, he abandoned all alcohol except for two glasses of wine with dinner every night. His weight then dropped to a healthy 200 pounds, his blood pressure improved, and he experienced a brief respite from the constant physical agony of the previous three years. But after Pauline's sudden death, he attacked the bottle more desperately than ever. Then, his skills as a writer disappeared. By 1958, he was working on *A Moveable Feast* and had resumed work on *The Garden of Eden*, which he had set aside in 1948. But he was having little success on either front. He managed to bring *A Moveable Feast* within sentences of completion before his ability to write vanished completely. Frozen with fear, he never convinced himself that the book was actually finished. It was published posthumously in 1964. Finally, Hemingway was becoming paranoid. The ever-present crowds made him distrustful. Anyone with a camera had suddenly become his enemy, after he had encouraged people to take photographs of his handsome face for decades. "You [photographers] are always trying to make a guy look foolish," he shouted during one familiar scene. "What are you trying to do? Get me with my mouth open? . . . I'm no movie star. Put away the camera."[12]

Hemingway's paranoia soon took a more political turn. In December of 1958, a Communist revolutionary named Fidel Castro ousted the oppressive government of General Fulgencio Batista in Cuba. As the choice of the nation's poor

Hemingway and the Cuban leader Fidel Castro in 1961. After 1945,
Hemingway settled in Cuba, but the Castro regime eventually forced him out of
the country.

and its workers, Castro drew from a broad base of support.
Just as Hemingway backed the popular Communist republic
in Spain in the 1930s, he now supported the new Castro
regime. He even considered Castro a friend. The two men had
gone fishing and drinking together on a few occasions. But his
willingness to support Castro, an enemy of the United States,
was not without consequences. FBI chief J. Edgar Hoover
took a renewed interest in Hemingway's public statements
after the Castro revolution—watching for signs of treason.
Of course, Hemingway remained loyal to his own nation, and
Hoover's concern was minor at best. Hemingway would have
been only a minor threat to American security if he had chosen Castro over the United States. But he was soon convinced
that his support for Castro had earned him important ene-

mies. In the late 1950s, he believed that the FBI was investigating his finances for signs of wrongdoing and that Hoover even sent out undercover agents to follow him through the streets of Cuba. Every man who sat near him in a restaurant became an FBI spy in Hemingway's eyes.

In the winter of 1958, Hemingway decided to buy a new house in the United States, to prove to the FBI that he was still a loyal American and to escape the violence of the Cuban revolution. In May of 1959, he bought a house for $50,000 in Ketchum, Idaho, one mile from Sun Valley in a pine forest at the foot of the Sawtooth Mountains, near Big Wood River. The modest Ketchum house was nothing like the regal mansions he owned in Cuba and in Key West. But it was a solid structure with windows offering a splendid view of the American heartland, seventeen acres of which were now Hemingway's. The move came at a good time. Finca Vigía was soon caught up in the middle of revolutionary fighting. Hemingway's favorite Labrador retriever, Black Dog, was killed by Batista troops searching the house for weapons. The house and most of Hemingway's books, paintings, cats, and hunting trophies were later confiscated by the Castro government in 1960.

In the summer of 1959, Hemingway was commissioned by *Life* magazine to write a 5,000 word article about the upcoming season of bullfights in Spain. He was paid $10,000 for his services. The assignment was an opportunity for Hemingway to escape from the pressures of his mounting paranoia. In addition, the *corrida* season promised to be an exciting one, as Hemingway's hero Antonio Ordóñez and his friend Luis Miguel Dominguín had challenged each other to a *mano a mano* duel—a series of bullfights in which two matadors fought six bulls and competed with each other for the most ear and tail trophies. Hemingway was given the chair of honor in the Pamplona grandstand for most of the contests, and both bullfighters dedicated their most difficult kills to

Hemingway, back in Spain in 1959 to cover the bullfights for Life *magazine, pours a glass of wine with some of the Pamplona locals.*

him. But he was still suffering from the plane crash injuries, and the paranoia, and he could not concentrate on his beloved spectacle. Then, during the bullfights one afternoon, Dominguín made a tragic mistake and was gored through the abdomen by a charging bull. Hemingway was inconsolable although Dominguín survived the tragedy. To boost his spirits, Mary threw Ernest a surprise sixtieth-birthday party, inviting all of his closest friends to Spain. She hired flamenco dancers, fireworks specialists, and set up a practice shooting range—where Hemingway shot a lit cigarette out of Antonio Ordónez's mouth. The party was a tremendous success, although Ernest and Mary later argued over its cost and Mary threatened to leave him for good.

After the summer festivals, the Hemingways sailed back to Finca Vigìa. They did not know that it would be their last stay in the crumbling mansion. Ordóñez accompanied them on the trip back to Cuba and Hemingway was happy, temporarily. But, when Ordóñez returned to Spain, Hemingway returned to his despondent, irritable ways. Then Mary broke her arm at the elbow and was not able to give her husband the attention he craved while she healed. In the summer of 1960, Hemingway returned to Spain aboard the ocean liner *Constitution*. Mary encouraged the trip as a way for Hemingway to escape his sad, inactive life in Cuba. He had already written 70,000 words for the *Life* article, 65,000 more than expected, and hoped to gather more information on this next trip to finish the article for good. Hemingway seldom left his hotel room, however, and the weeks in Spain passed with agonizing slowness. Some people thought that he was overworked, that the *mano a mano* article was wearing him down. But Mary knew that her husband was finally succumbing to the depression that had been building for decades. On September 2, the first installment of his long-awaited article, "The Dangerous Summer," appeared in *Life* magazine. Hemingway's picture once again appeared on the front cover, but this time Hemingway was disturbed by the aging face he saw there. On September 25, he sent Mary a letter that seemed to hold out all the hope he had left:

> *Lots of problems but we will solve them all. Not sleeping, tricky memory, etc. bad—any drinking bad for me except lightest claret. Plenty others but will work them out and I'll get healthy and write fine.*[13]

The letter was optimistic, but no one believed that Hemingway's return to productive life would be that easy—not even Hemingway.

He returned to New York in the fall of 1960, a badly damaged man. Ironically for a man who once prided himself

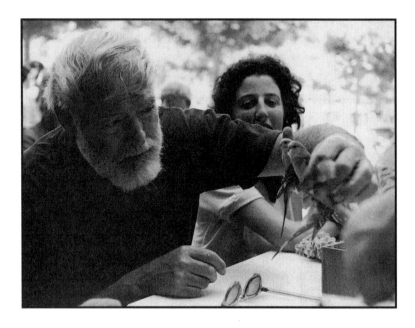

The excitement of the bullfights in Pamplona in 1959 did little to lift the spirits of Hemingway, who had difficulty writing and increasingly suffered from depression in his old age.

on his "'fraid of nothin'" attitude, fear was now the dominant characteristic of his personality. Mary could not get him to leave their New York hotel room. Then, in Chicago, he retreated from all contact with strangers. And finally, at his home in Ketchum, his fears of the FBI returned. Mary no longer had the strength to help her husband. His problems were simply too severe for her tough brand of home care. A. E. Hotchner therefore suggested that she send him for professional help. As much as she hated to admit it, Mary now knew that Hotchner was right. Of course, Hemingway refused to seek psychiatric help at first. He fought stubbornly against the suggestion that he check himself into the Menninger Clinic, the best psychiatric hospital in the nation.

The news of his stay at Menninger would ripple through the gossip channels and cause him unnecessary humiliation. "They'll say I'm losing my marbles," Hemingway said.[14] Mary then decided that she would only bring her husband to a hospital that treated both psychological and physical ailments. That way, she reasoned, the newspapers and Hemingway himself could only guess at the true nature of his ailments. Within a week, Hemingway was admitted into the Mayo Clinic in Rochester, Minnesota. He was told that the doctors were treating his high blood pressure. When the painful electroshock therapy began, however, he knew that Mary and his friends had lied. Like Ezra Pound and Scott Fitzgerald before him, he was experiencing his own mental collapse. And a proud man like Ernest Hemingway could not live with that knowledge for very long.

"DESTROYED BUT NOT DEFEATED"

CHAPTER X

The gong rang and Jack turned quick and went out. Walcott came toward him and they touched gloves and as soon as Walcott dropped his hands Jack jumped his left into his face twice. There wasn't anybody ever boxed better than Jack.

—Fifty Grand

ERNEST HEMINGWAY WAS always more comfortable on the attack. He did not like to defend his work against criticism, but he would maliciously criticize the work of his friends. He craved human contact, but he was usually responsible for the collapse of his friendships and his marriages. He lived intensely, dangerously, surviving bomb explosions, plane crashes, hunting accidents, revolutions, and an extraordinary number of barfights. But then came the psychological collapse, and he found himself checking into the Mayo Clinic under an assumed name. He was no longer on the attack. (He signed into the clinic as George Saviens, adopting the name of his Idaho medical doctor.) Mary suggested the name change as a way to ward off the press while her husband to began his recovery. In happier times, Hemingway might not have adopted such a sneaky method of self-protection. He had swaggered into dozens of hospitals in his life, always using his quick wit and heroic persona to take the emphasis away from

Hemingway and Mary at their home at Finca Vigìa, near Havana, Cuba, in 1959.

his injuries. But he was no longer capable of putting on a show. In 1960, as he entered the Mayo Clinic, Hemingway began his retreat from life.

Even as he was being admitted into the clinic, Hemingway had only a vague notion of what was to come. Mary maintained that he was going to be treated for high-blood pressure and a developing case of diabetes. Doctors supported Mary's claim and took Hemingway off his blood pressure medicine—which may have been contributing to his depression. But once he had settled into the routine of the clinic, the doctors and Mary told him the truth. His greatest fears had come true. He was going to be treated for the deterioration of his mind, the source of his livelihood. But the treatment was even worse than the diagnosis. The doctors put Hemingway through a number of grueling treatments of electroshock therapy, sending strong doses of electrical current through his brain in the hope of restoring his capacities to think and act rationally. This method of treatment was still in the developmental stages in the early 1960s, and the doses Hemingway received were probably incorrect. After a few treatments, he began to experience the dreaded side effect: memory loss.

When Hemingway noticed the forgetfulness for the first time, his attitude toward the Mayo Clinic and his treatment changed from one of embarrassment and anger to one of despair. He lost all hope of returning to his writing career. As his brother Leicester remembers:

> [Doctors] went heavily into shock therapy which they probably thought was going to fix him up immediately, and I don't think they did a good enough job of assuring him that his memory was going to come back. Because what scared the bejesus out of him was the realization it had wiped out so much of his memory.[1]

Like many of the characters in his books, Hemingway still had a lot of good stories to write. But he no longer had the mental capacity to call those stories up in his mind.

By January of 1960, he was certain that he had experienced a writer's death. And then the world press had finally caught up with Hemingway's hospitalization. Newspaper headlines announced the latest theories about the famous writer's mysterious illness. Hemingway once again feared the onslaught of publicity, and friends were concerned that his outlook was becoming dangerously gloomy. Some hoped that an invitation to the upcoming Inaugural Ball in Washington, D.C., would take his mind off of his medical status. President-elect John F. Kennedy—who had just defeated Richard Nixon in the race to the Oval Office—heard about Hemingway's illness and sent a letter to the Mayo Clinic requesting his presence at the celebration. Hemingway was gratified to be remembered by the young Kennedy, but he was too sick and too ashamed of his present condition to accept the invitation.

He was not too sick, however, to convince his doctors that he was ready to return home. On January 22, 1961, after telling the doctors exactly what they wanted to hear about his own recovery, Hemingway was sent back to Ketchum. During a brief stay at home, he tried unsuccessfully to recover the fragments of his normal life. The paranoia and the violent temper returned, the writing ability never did. Hemingway agonized for hours over a single sentence in his *A Moveable Feast* manuscript. When he finally gave up, he had nothing to show for his work. As usual, he took his disappointment out on Mary and made himself impossible to live with. But he was too ashamed of his condition to face the outside world. As Gregory Hemingway remembers, even his sons were left in the dark about his situation:

> *That my father would tell me the truth about his mental illness was unthinkable. Something physical, sure. But mental, never. He was too much my father, my model, a whole generation's model, and he thought he'd fail those whom he had wanted so desperately to teach, had tried all his life to teach.*[2]

Hemingway's fear of failure then turned to desperation. One day, not long after his return to Ketchum, Mary found Ernest holding a loaded shotgun. Knowing how his illness was advancing, she feared that she had walked in on a suicide attempt. Maintaining a steady, calm voice, she successfully talked the weapon out of Hemingway's hands and arranged his readmission to the Mayo Clinic.

On the day of his return trip to Rochester, Minnesota, before leaving for the airport, a friend found Hemingway in the Ketchum house once again holding a loaded shotgun. The man wrestled Hemingway to the floor before the desperate writer gave up the gun. By some accounts, the flight from Idaho to Minnesota was equally difficult, with Hemingway trying to open the plane's cabin door midway through the flight, and even trying to throw himself into the plane's moving propellers as he waited on a runway during a refueling stop. But he finally arrived safely at the clinic and was immediately enrolled in the closed ward of St. Mary's Hospital, in a sterile cell with barred windows. After a few more weeks in relative isolation, and a second round of electroshock therapy, Hemingway succeeded again in convincing the doctors that he would be able to function in the outside world. Mary fought the doctors' decision, but he was released anyway.

The weeks following Hemingway's first suicide attempts were long and miserable. Hemingway no longer seemed to take an active interest in his own well-being. The electroshock therapy sapped him of his strength and of his will to fight. He looked different physically as well—frail, thin, and hollow. Worst of all, he knew that he was a different person now and could do nothing about it. For a time, he seemed to accept his new role as the retired champion of the literary world. But this apparent resignation was his final lie. On July 1, 1961 Ernest, Mary, and a friend went out to dinner. Hemingway scared his companions when he claimed to see yet another FBI agent stalking him, but for the most part it was an uneventful evening. That night, Mary put Ernest to bed in his own bedroom and sang him an Italian song that he loved. Then she went to bed. Early the next morning, Hemingway woke up and walked down into the basement. He found the keys to his gun-cabinet. He went to his cabinet and pulled out his favorite double-barreled hunting shotgun. Then he climbed the stairs back into the house, put the shotgun to his head and pulled the trigger. After numerous failed attempts to commit suicide following the loss of his writing ability, Ernest Hemingway succeeded on July 2, 1961—a few weeks before his sixty-first birthday.

Ketchum, the Hemingway home in Idaho, where, after several failed attempts, Hemingway took his own life on July 2, 1961.

He was buried a few days later during a small, private ceremony. His grave rests in an ordinary plot in Ketchum cemetery, at the foot of the Sawtooth Mountains, in a prairie running flat to the mountain peaks.

When Ernest Hemingway wrote "a man can be destroyed but not defeated," he was at the top of his form. In fact, he was just about to win the Pulitzer and Nobel Prizes and was completing what is arguably the most-popular story of the twentieth century, *The Old Man and the Sea.* He already had three major novels under his belt—*The Sun Also Rises, A Farewell to Arms*, and *For Whom the Bell Tolls*—as well as a revolutionary collection of short stories—*In Our Time*—and a number of individual short stories to rival anything ever written in the English language—including "The Snows of Kilimanjaro," "The Short Happy Life of Francis Macomber," and "A Clean Well-Lighted Place." He had created a new writing style for the modern age, and he was also very confident that his accomplishments rated him a place among a very select group of writers in the history of world literature:

> *I started out very quiet and I beat Mr. Turgenev. Then I tried very hard and I beat Mr. de Maupassant. I've fought two draws with Mr. Stendhal and I think I had the edge in the last one. But nobody's going to get me in the ring with Mr. Tolstoy unless I'm crazy or I keep getting better.*[3]

There was reason for optimism in the early 1950s. Although *Across the River and Into the Trees* was a critical and popular failure, Hemingway was still writing well enough to produce a classic. And he was still an engaging character, even if he was too old for the excitement of war and the intrusions of the popular media. He probably had no idea that Santiago's now-famous line, "A man can be destroyed but not defeated," would become an apt phrase for describing his own legacy.

After the first round of electroshock therapy, Hemingway was a destroyed man. Papa—the swashbuckling veteran of wars, the courageous sportsman, the charismatic celebrity, the world-renowned artist—had become a feeble, bitter, and disturbed shell of his past glory. He then committed the act he had called "selfish" years earlier. He took his own life. But he has never been defeated. His books and stories are the proof of his victory. They are still among the most important and popular creations of American culture. Hemingway has joined the exclusive list of America's literary masters—

Hawthorne, Poe, Whitman, Dickinson, Twain, and Faulkner. His major works—three novels, a novella, and a group of short stories—are American classics. But his minor works are also widely read. They too are a testament to his lasting reputation and his superb writing style, and to the engaging Hemingway personality that shines through every word on the page. Even among nonliterary circles, the Hemingway name continues to describe a way of life—the "code" of his characters as well as the hard-living, adventure-seeking existence that he actually lived.

But before Hemingway became a cultural icon, he was a living, breathing man with a family that has carried his name into future generations. His first son, Bumby, left the army after years of distinguished service and became a stock broker in California. Patrick graduated with honors from Harvard University and later became a professional hunter in Africa. And Gregory, after his stormy teenage years, went on to graduate from medical school and set up his own medical practice. All three sons would have their own battles with alcohol, like their father, but they also would succeed in raising families and living relatively normal lives after their unusual childhoods. Bumby's beautiful daughters, Mariel and Margaux, have even carved out their own celebrity status in recent years as television and movie actresses.

Of course their grandfather was no stranger to allure of Hollywood. Hemingway's legacy within American culture is well documented in film and television. It is apparent in the sheer number of times Hollywood has attempted to adapt his stories to the screen and in the actors who fought to play his characters. After Helen Hayes and Gary Cooper teamed up in the movie version of *A Farewell to Arms* in 1937, a short list of the Hemingway films for the large screen includes *The Killers* starring Burt Lancaster and Ava Gardner, *The Snows of Kilimanjaro* starring Gregory Peck, *The Macomber Affair* starring Robert Preston, a second *A Farewell to Arms* starring Rock

Hudson and Jennifer Jones, *For Whom the Bell Tolls* starring Ingrid Bergman and Gary Cooper, Spencer Tracy's *The Old Man and the Sea*, and Errol Flynn in *The Sun Also Rises*. Hemingway's work also enjoyed a certain amount of success on the small screen. His biographer A. E. Hotchner was responsible for a great many of the television adaptations that appeared in the 1950s, attracting such talented actors as Richard Burton and Jason Robards as well as a young actor named Paul Newman. By far the strangest idea for a Hemingway story was set into motion in 1951, when a group of admirers put together a ballet adaptation of the story "The Capital of the World." William Faulkner and F. Scott Fitzgerald both worked as script writers in Hollywood later in their careers. But Hemingway, a Hollywood outsider, was writing the actual stories that the American public wanted to see performed.

Like his life, Hemingway's legacy extends beyond the borders of his native country. He remains a legendary figure in Spain, a war hero as well as a grand figure in the history of the bullfight. In such books as *The Sun Also Rises* and *Death in the Afternoon*, Hemingway introduced the beauty and pageantry of the *corrida* to millions of readers all over the world. Thanks to his ringing endorsements of Spanish culture, the once-quiet city of Pamplona has been transformed into a bustling center of tourism, especially during the summer festivals. A stone bust of the great writer now stands in the center of town.

There is another Hemingway bust in the Cuban village of Cojimar, the village made famous in *The Old Man and the Sea*. When Hemingway died, every fisherman in the village donated a brass fitting from his boat to a local sculptor, who then melted the metal and cast it into the famous face of "Mr. Ernesto." The bust is the centerpiece of a seaside monument known as Plaza Hemingway. Another bust watches over Hemingway's favorite bar in the Havana restaurant El

Floridita. Hemingway's name has been given to a species of Carribean porpoise, *Neoreminthe Hemingway*, and the Cuban rum, "El Ron Vigìa" is named after his home. The Castro government has also renamed a Havana marina after the great writer and continues to preserve the Finca Vigìa as a tourist attraction, and a much needed source of income. *Pilar*, too, is preserved in a pavilion near the house, in San Francisco de Paula. And *Pilar's* second mate, ninety-six-year-old Gregorio Fuentes, continues to fight for his captain's honor. He still protects Hemingway's memory from the visitors who are too quick to criticize Hemingway's lifestyle. Fuentes remains a minor celebrity in Cuba, more than thirty years after Hemingway's death.[4]

But if any city has fought to keep the Hemingway spirit alive, it is Key West. The author's face graces the T-shirts sold at his favorite drinking place, Sloppy Joe's, which is now a major American tourist attraction. Hemingway's house on Whitehead Street is a national landmark. Tour books are printed yearly so that visitors can follow Papa's own footsteps through the island that was his home for twelve years. And every summer, Hemingway fans from all over the world congregate on the island for a week-long celebration of Hemingway's legacy, "Hemingway Days." The celebration includes a fishing tournament, a sailing regatta, countless stops at Sloppy Joe's, and the now-famous Hemingway look-alike contest—the favorite event of heavy-set, bearded men everywhere. As one of the participants in "Hemingway Days" says, there is more at stake in the look-alike contests and the fishing tournaments than a simple admiration for the great writer:

> One of the things so difficult for [the Hemingway fanatics] is their wives think it's kind of silly. The wives may not really understand how much it means to us, not to look like him but to be involved in the whole culture.[5]

Indeed, Hemingway's name has come to represent an entire culture, a masculine world of hard living and fast action. Most fans choose not to remember that the hard life and the action later took a fatal toll on their hero, but it is truly amazing that a literary figure continues to excite the American imagination so many decades after his death.

In July of 1961, Hemingway was a destroyed man. But he has risen from the ashes of his death and remains the undefeated literary champion of the twentieth century. He is a permanent feature of American culture. As he predicted in *The Green Hills of Africa*, his legacy has survived changing tastes in literature, wars, political changes, and technological innovations, and he continues to influence the way we think about love and war, hunting and fishing, men and women, and the abiding power of words:

> *A country finally erodes and the dust blows away, the people all die and none of them were of any importance permanently, except those who practiced the arts.*[6]

NOTES

CHAPTER 1

1. Kenneth S. Lynn, *Hemingway* (New York: Simon and Schuster, 1987), p. 69.
2. Ibid., p. 176.
3. Ernest Hemingway, *The Complete Short Stories of Ernest Hemingway: The Finca Vigìa Edition* (New York: Charles Scribner's Sons, 1987), p. 337.
4. Peter Griffin, *Along With Youth: Hemingway, The Early Years* (New York: Oxford University Press, 1985), p. 70.
5. Ibid., p. 73.
6. Griffin, p. 74.
7. Ernest Hemingway, *A Farewell to Arms* (New York: Scribner's, 1957), p. 52.
8. Griffin, p. 76.
9. Archibald MacLeish, "His Mirror Was Danger," *Life* magazine, July 14, 1961, p. 71.

CHAPTER 2

1. Ernest Hemingway, *The Green Hills of Africa* (New York: Scribner's, 1963), pp. 70–71.
2. Marcelline Hemingway Sanford, *At the Hemingways: A Family*

Portrait (Boston: Atlantic Monthly Press, 1962), p. 23.

3. Ibid., p. 61.

4. James R. Mellow, *Hemingway: A Life Without Consequences* (New York: Houghton Mifflin Company, 1992), p. 6.

5. Ibid., p. 6.

6. Sanford, p. 6.

7. Mellow, p. 12.

8. Charles A. Fenton, *The Apprenticeship of Ernest Hemingway: The Early Years* (New York: The Viking Press, 1954), p. 1.

9. Kenneth S. Lynn, *Hemingway*, (New York: Simon and Schuster, 1985), p. 3

10. A. E. Hotchner, *Hemingway and His World* (New York: Vendome Press, 1989), p. 15.

11. Jeffery Meyers, *Hemingway: A Biography* (New York: Harper and Row Publishers, 1985), p. 19.

12. Mellow, p. 42.

13. Matthew J. Bruccoli, ed. *Ernest Hemingway, Cub Reporter: Kansas City Star Stories* (Pittsburg: University of Pittsburg Press, 1970), p. 28.

14. Mellow, p. 45.

CHAPTER 3

1. A. E. Hotchner, "Hemingway Talks to American Youth," in *Conversations with Ernest Hemingway*, ed. Matthew J. Bruccoli (Jackson: University Press of Mississippi, 1986), p. 146.

2. James R. Mellow, *Hemingway: A Life Without Consequences* (New York: Houghton Mifflin Company, 1992), p. 63.

3. Ibid., p. 61.

4. Henry S. Villard and James Nagel, eds. *Hemingway in Love and War: The Lost Diary of Agnes von Kurowsky, Her Letters and Correspondence of Ernest Hemingway* (Boston: Northeastern University Press, 1989), p. 72.

5. Ibid., p. 73.

6. Ibid., p. 149.
7. Michael Reynolds, *The Young Hemingway* (New York: Basil Blackwell, Inc. 1986), p. 19.
8. Mellor, p. 88.
9. Ibid., p. 90.
10. William White, ed. *Ernest Hemingway, Dateline Toronto: The Complete Toronto Star Dispatches 1920–1924* (New York: Charles Scribner's Sons, 1985), p. 8.
11. Gioia Dilberto, *Hadley* (New York: Ticknor and Fields, 1992), pp. 60–61.
12. Ibid., p. 48.
13. Ibid., p. 93.
14. Villard, p. 164.

CHAPTER 4

1. A. E. Hotchner, *Hemingway and His World* (New York: Vendome Press, 1989), p. 50.
2. Ernest Hemingway, *Ernest Hemingway: Selected Letters 1917–1961*, ed. Carlos Baker (New York: Charles Scribner's Sons, 1981), p. 59.
3. Ernest Hemingway, *A Moveable Feast* (New York: Charles Scribner's Sons, 1964), p. 14.
4. Jeffrey Meyers, *Hemingway: A Biography* (New York: Harper and Row Publishers, 1985), p. 74.
5. Hemingway, *A Moveable Feast*, p. 110.
6. James R. Mellow, *Hemingway: A Life Without Consequences* (New York: Houghton Mifflin Company, 1992), p. 175.
7. Ibid., p. 160.
8. William White, ed. *Dateline Toronto: The Complete Toronto Star Dispatches 1920–1924* (New York: Charles Scribner's Sons, 1985), p. 232.
9. Ibid., p. 173.
10. Ibid., p. 255.
11. Mellor, p. 201.
12. Ibid., p. 234.

13. Hemingway, *Selected Letters*, pp. 92–93.

14. Ibid., p. 153.

15. Robert Manning, "Hemingway in Cuba," in *Conversations with Ernest Hemingway*, ed. Matthew J. Bruccoli (Jackson: University Press of Mississippi, 1986), p. 182.

16. Jed Kiley, *Hemingway: An Old Friend Remembers* (New York: Hawthorn Books, 1965), p. 33.

17. Ibid. p. 58.

18. Ibid. p. 24.

CHAPTER 5

1. James R. Mellor, *Hemingway: A Life Without Consequences* (New York; Houghton Mifflin Compay, 1992), p. 317.

2. Hemingway, Ernest, *The Hemingway Reader*, ed. Charles Poore (New York: Charles Scribner's Sons, 1953), p. 30.

3. Ernest Hemingway, *Ernest Hemingway: Selected Letters 1917–1961*, ed. Carlos Baker (New York: Charles Scribner's Sons, 1981), p. 221.

4. Fraser Drew, "April 8, 1955 with Ernest Hemingway: Unedited Notes on a Visit to Finca Vigìa" in *Conversations with Ernest Hemingway*, ed. Matthew J. Bruccoli (Jackson: University Press of Mississippi, 1986), p. 94.

5. Jeffrey Meyers, *Hemingway: A Biography* (New York: Harper and Row Publishers, 1985), p. 185.

6. Mellor, p. 340.

7. Ernest Hemingway, *A Moveable Feast* (New York: Collier Books, 1964), p. 210.

8. Mellor, p. 336.

9. Hemingway, *Selected Letters*, p. 205.

10. Mellor, p. 352.

11. Ibid. p. 357.

12. Meyers, p. 208.

13. Robert Manning, "Hemingway in Cuba" in Bruccoli, p. 184.

CHAPTER 6

1. Ernest Hemingway, *A Farewell to Arms* (New York: Charles Scribner's Sons, 1929), p. 185.
2. Ernest Hemingway, *Ernest Hemingway: Selected Letters 1917–1961,* ed. Carlos Baker (New York: Charles Scribner's Sons, 1981), p. 297.
3. Jed Kiley, *Hemingway: An Old Friend Remembers* (New York: Hawthorn Books Inc. 1965), p. 59.
4. A. E. Hotchner, *Hemingway and His World* (New York: Vendome Press, 1989), p. 105.
5. James Mellow, *Hemingway: A Life Without Consequences* (New York: Houghton Mifflin Company, 1992), p. 390.
6. Gregory Hemingway, *Papa: A Personal Memoir* (Boston: Houghton Mifflin Company, 1976), p. 19.
7. Mellow, p. 415.
8. Ibid., p. 415.
9. Hotchner, p. 113.
10. Hemingway, p. 402.
11. Gregory Hemingway, p. 18.
12. Hotchner, p. 124.
13. Stuart B. McIver, *Hemingway's Key West* (Sarasota, FL: Pineapple Press Inc., 1993), p. 42.
14. Gregory Hemingway, p. 29.
15. George Plimpton, "The Art of Fiction" in *Conversations with Ernest Hemingway,* ed. Matthew J. Bruccoli (Jackson: University Press of Mississippi, 1986), p. 123.
16. Mellow, p. 441.
17. Hemingway, p. 419.

CHAPTER 7

1. James R. Mellos, *Hemingway: A Life Without Consequences* (New York: Houghton Mifflin Company, 1992), p. 481.
2. Ernest Hemingway, *To Have and Have Not* (New York: Charles Scribner's Sons, 1937), p. 224.

3. Ibid., title page.

4. Ernest Hemingway, *Ernest Hemingway: Selected Letters 1917–1961*, ed. Carlos Baker (New York: Charles Scribner's Sons, 1981), p. 457.

5. Mellow, p. 496.

6. Denis Brian, *The True Gen: An Intimate Portrait of Hemingway By Those Who Knew Him* (New York: Grove Press, 1988), p. 115.

7. Ibid., p. 118.

8. Mellow, p. 499.

9. Robert Manning, "Hemingway in Cuba" in *Conversations with Ernest Hemingway*, ed. Matthew J. Bruccoli (Jackson: University Press of Mississippi, 1986), p. 182.

10. Hemingway, *Selected Letters*, pp. 463–64

11. Robert Van Gelder, "Ernest Hemingway Talks of Work and War" in Bruccoli, p. 17.

12. Hemingway, *Selected Letters*, p. 503.

CHAPTER 8

1. Ernest Hemingway, *Ernest Hemingway: Selected Letters 1917–1961*, ed. Carlos Baker (New York: Charles Scribner's Sons, 1981), p. 527.

2. Denis Brian, *The True Gen: An Intimate Portrait of Hemingway By Those Who Knew Him* (New York: Grove Press, 1988), pp. 139–140.

3. Gregory H. Hemingway, *Papa: A Personal Memoir* (Boston: Houghton Mifflin Company, 1976), p. 89.

4. James R. Mellow, *Hemingway: A Life Without Consequences* (New York: Houghton Mifflin Company, 1992), p. 530.

5. Ibid., p. 530.

6. Brian, p. 155.

7. Mellow, p. 539.

8. A. E. Hotchner, *Hemingway and His World* (New York: Vendome Press, 1989), pp. 112–113.

9. Harvey Breit, "Talk with Mr. Hemingway" in *Conversations with Ernest Hemingway*, ed. Matthew J. Bruccoli (Jackson: University Press of Mississippi, 1986), pp. 61–62.

CHAPTER 9

1. Ernest Hemingway, *The Old Man and the Sea* (New York: Collier Books, 1952), p. 103.
2. "His final chapter to a magnificent story magnificently told," *Life* magazine, July 14, 1961, p. 2.
3. Matthew J. Bruccoli, *Conversations with Ernest Hemingway* (Jackson: University Press of Mississippi, 1986), p. ix.
4. "His final chapter to a magnificent story magnificently told," p. 2.
5. James R. Mellow, *Hemingway: A Life Without Consequences* (New York: Houghton Mifflin Company, 1992), p. 582.
6. "His final chapter to a magnificent story magnificently told," p. 2.
7. A. E. Hotchner, *Papa Hemingway* (New York: Random House, 1966), p. 87.
8. Mellow, pp. 589–590.
9. Ernest Hemingway, *Ernest Hemingway: Selected Letters 1917–1961*, ed. Carlos Baker (New York; Charles Scribner's Sons, 1981), p. 843.
10. Ernest Hemingway, *A Moveable Feast* (New York: Collier Books, 1964), preface.
11. Hotchner, p. 150.
12. Milt Machlin, "Hemingway Talking" in Bruccoli, p. 134.
13. Hemingway, *Selected Letters*, p. 908.
14. Mellow, p. 601.

CHAPTER 10

1. Denis Brian, *The True Gen: An Intimate Portrait of Hemingway By Those Who Knew Him* (New York: Grove Press, 1988), p. 252.
2. Gregroy H. Hemingway, *Papa: A Personal Memoir* (Boston: Houghton Mifflin Company, 1986), p. 115.
3. Matthew J. Bruccoli, ed., *Conversations with Ernest Hemingway* (Jackson: University Press of Mississippi, 1986), p. x.
4. Larry Smith, "He Fights for Hemingway," *Parade Magazine*, July 2, 1995, p. 8.
5. Amy Wu, "Prodigal Papa Returns," *Florida Herald*, July 23, 1995, p. 2B.
6. Ernest Hemingway, *The Green Hills of Africa* (New York: Collier Books, 1935), p. 109.

BIOGRAPHICAL
TIMELINE

July 21, 1899   Ernest Hemingway is born in Oak Park, Illinois, the first son of Clarence Edmonds Hemingway and Grace Hall Hemingway.

1917   Hemingway graduates from Oak Park High School but refuses to go to college. He takes a reporting job in Kansas City.

June 18, 1918   As an ambulance driver in Italy during World War I, Hemingway is wounded and falls in love with his nurse Agnes von Kurowsky.

1920   Hemingway moves to Toronto as a tutor, then as a reporter for the *Toronto Star*. Back in Chicago, he meets Hadley Richardson, who becomes his first wife.

1921   Hemingway arrives in Paris to begin his writing career among the great writers of the expatriate movement, including

Gertrude Stein, Ezra Pound, James Joyce, and F. Scott Fitzgerald.

1923   Hemingway's first book, *Three Stories and Ten Poems*, is published by a small, private press. It is followed by the vignette collection *in our time*.

1925   The first Hemingway classic, *In Our Time*, is published to rave reviews.

1926   Scribner's publishes *Torrents of Spring*, and then Hemingway's first popular success, *The Sun Also Rises*.

1927   Hemingway divorces Hadley and marries Pauline Pfeiffer.

1929   *A Farewell to Arms* is published and Hemingway becomes America's new literary hero.

1932   Scribner's publishes Hemingway's tribute to the Spanish bullfights, *Death in the Afternoon*. Then he takes part in an African safari, the future setting of *The Green Hills of Africa*, "The Snows of Kilimanjaro," and "The Short Happy Life of Francis Macomber."

1937   With reporter Martha Gellhorn, Hemingway travels to Spain to cover the civil war for a group of newspapers. Later, he divorces Pauline and marries Martha Gellhorn.

1940	Hemingway's greatest novel, *For Whom the Bell Tolls*, is published to enormous popular success. He and Martha travel to China to cover the Sino-Japanese War.
1942	Hemingway creates a spy ring in the Caribbean islands and then searches for German submarines in contribution to America's effort in World War II.
1944	Hemingway arrives in Europe as a war reporter, takes part in the final battles of World War II, and meets Mary Welsh, his fourth wife.
1952	*The Old Man and the Sea*, Hemingway's first success since 1940, appears in *Life* magazine. The book will earn Hemingway a Pulitzer Prize and the 1954 Noble Prize for Literature.
1953	On safari in Africa, Hemingway is involved in two plane crashes in two days and suffers a number of lingering injuries, which haunt him for the rest of his life.
1960	Hemingway is admitted into the Mayo Clinic for a psychological evaluation and treatment for severe depression and paranoia.
July 2, 1961	Hemingway commits suicide in his house in Ketchum, Idaho.

BIBLIOGRAPHY

Baker, Christopher. "Papa's Cuba." *New York Daily News*, September 3, 1995.

Brian, Denis. *The True Gen: An Intimate Portrait of Hemingway By Those Who Knew Him.* New York: Grove Press, 1988.

Bruccoli, Matthew J., ed. *Conversations with Ernest Hemingway* Jackson: University Press of Mississippi, 1986.

Bruccoli, Matthew J., ed. *Ernest Hemingway, Cub Reporter: Kansas City Star Stories.* Pittsburg: University of Pittsburg Press, 1970.

Castillo-Puche, José-Luis. *Hemingway in Spain.* Garden City, NY: Doubleday and Co., 1974.

Dilberto, Gioia. *Hadley.* New York: Ticknor and Fields, 1992.

Fenton, Charles A. *The Apprenticeship of Ernest Hemingway: The Early Years.* New York: The Viking Press, 1954.

Fitch, Noel Riley. *Walks in Hemingway's Paris.* New York: St. Martin's Press, 1989.

Griffin, Peter. *Along With Youth: Hemingway, The Early Years*. New York: Oxford University Press, 1985.

Hemingway Ernest. *Ernest Hemingway: Selected Letters 1917–1961*. Edited by Carlos Baker. New York: Charles Scribner's Sons, 1981.

Hemingway, Gregory H. *Papa: A Personal Memoir*. Boston: Houghton Mifflin Company, 1976.

"His final chapter to a magnificent story magnificently told." *Life* magazine, July 14, 1961.

Hotchner, A. E. *Hemingway and His World*. New York: Vendome Press, 1989.

————. *Papa Hemingway*. New York: Random House, 1966.

Kiley, Jed. *Hemingway: An Old Friend Remembers*. New York: Hawthorn Books, 1965.

Lynn, Kenneth S. *Hemingway*. New York: Simon and Schuster, 1987.

Lyttle, Richard B. *Ernest Hemingway: The Life and the Legend*. New York: MacMillian Children's Group, 1992.

McDowell, N. *Hemingway*. New York: Chelsea House, 1989.

McIver, Stuart B. *Hemingway's Key West*. Sarasota, FL: Pineapple Press, 1993.

MacLeish, Archibald. "His Mirror Was Danger." *Life* magazine, July 14, 1961.

McLendon, James. *Papa: Hemingway in Key West*. Miami: E. A. Seemann Publishing, 1972.

Mellow, James R. *Hemingway: A Life Without Consequences*. New York: Houghton Mifflin Company, 1992.

Meyers, Jeffrey. *Hemingway: A Biography*. New York: Harper and Row Publishers, 1985.

————. *The Hemingway Reader*. Edited by Charles Poore. New York: Charles Scribner's Sons, 1953.

Reynolds, Michael. *The Young Hemingway*. New York: Basil Blackwell, 1986.

Rovit, Earl. *Ernest Hemingway*. Boston: Twayne Publishers, 1963.

Sanford, Marcelline Hemingway. *At the Hemingway's: A Family Portrait*. Boston: Atlantic Monthly Press, 1962.

Smith, Larry. "He Fights for Hemingway." *Parade* magazine, July 2, 1995.

Villard, Henry S. *Hemingway in Love and War: The Lost Diary of Agnes von Kurowsky, Her Letters and Correspondence of Ernest Hemingway*. Edited by James Nagel. Boston: Northeastern University Press, 1989.

Wagner, Linda Welshimer. *Ernest Hemingway: Five Decades of Criticism*. Ann Arbor: Michigan State University Press, 1974.

White, William, ed. *Dateline Toronto: The Complete Toronto Star Dispatches 1920–1924*. New York: Charles Scribner's Sons, 1985.

Wu, Amy. "Prodigal Papa Returns." *Florida Herald*, July 23, 1995.

Suggested Reading

The Sun Also Rises. New York: Collier Books, 1926.

A Farewell to Arms. New York: Collier Books, 1929.

For Whom the Bell Tolls. New York: Collier Books, 1940.

The Old Man and the Sea. New York: Collier Books, 1952.

A Moveable Feast. New York: Collier Books, 1964.

The Complete Short Stories of Ernest Hemingway: The Finca Vigìa Edition. New York: Charles Scribner's Sons, 1987.

John Tessitore is a recent graduate of Harvard University, where he studied history and English literature. He is a regular contributor to the Christian Science Monitor.

INDEX